really easy piano

T0003521

40 POP SONGS FOR KIDS

ISBN: 978-1-70511-395-0

Visit Hal Leonard Online at
www.halleonard.com

Contact us:
Hal Leonard
7777 West Bluemound Road
Milwaukee, WI 53213
Email: info@halleonard.com

In Europe, contact:
Hal Leonard Europe Limited
42 Wigmore Street
Marylebone, London, W1U 2RY
Email: info@halleonardeurope.com

In Australia, contact:
Hal Leonard Australia Pty. Ltd.
4 Lentara Court
Cheltenham, Victoria, 3192 Australia
Email: info@halleonard.com.au

40 POP SONGS FOR KIDS

Adore You

Words and Music by Harry Styles, Thomas Hull, Tyler Johnson and Amy Allen

This track comes from Harry Styles' second solo album, *Fine Line*, released in 2019. The singer was originally part of One Direction, who were formed as part of the 2010 UK series of the talent show, X Factor. Since their breakup in 2015, Harry Styles has gone on to have a successful solo career. This track features a quirky music video directed by Dave Meyers, where Styles adopts a little fish that ends up growing so large, he has to release it into the ocean!

Hints & Tips: In the verse, the high phrases in the right hand should sound like echoes; play these softer. Keep your wrist relaxed to play the quick repeated notes, eg. bar 13.

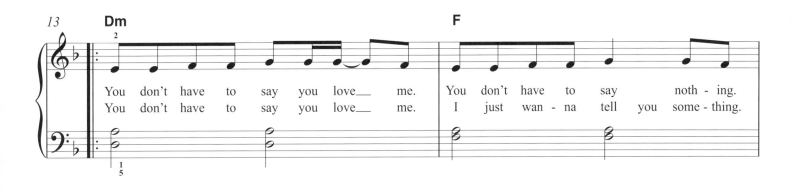

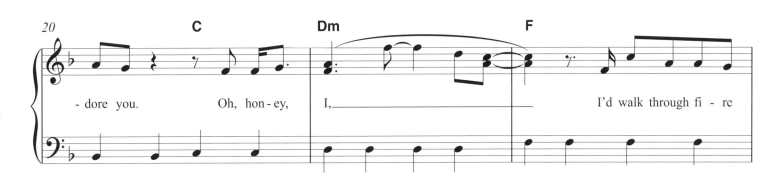

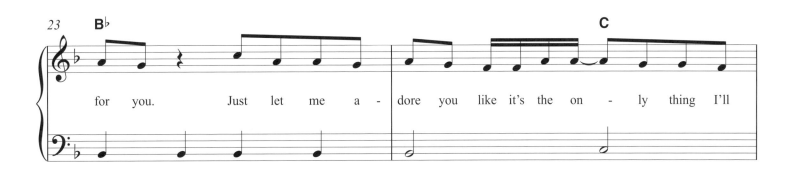

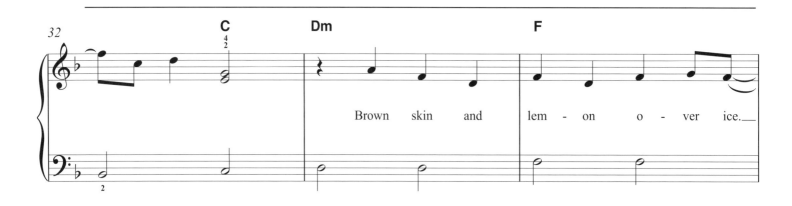

Bad Day

Words and Music by Daniel Powter

Daniel Powter released this single from his self-titled 2005 album and hit the No. 2 spot in the UK and No. 1 in the US. It is Powter's only big hit to date – his later releases did not meet the same acclaim as 'Bad Day'. The music video featured Samaire Armstrong, who starred in popular American teen drama, *The O.C.*, at the time the song was released. The song was used by TV show *American Idol* as their elimination song for a time, while fans watched a farewell montage of the defeated contestant!

Hints & Tips: Practise the right hand on its own first to get the hang of the 'shuffle' rhythm in the melody line. Keeping the tempo slow will help.

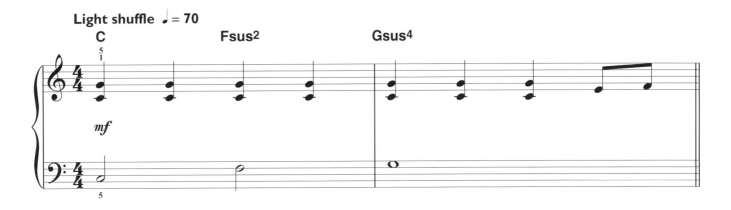

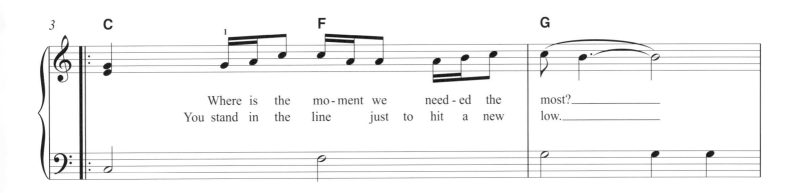

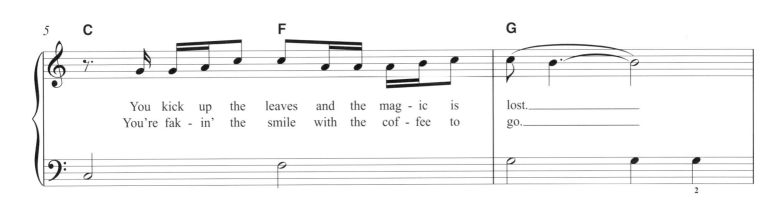

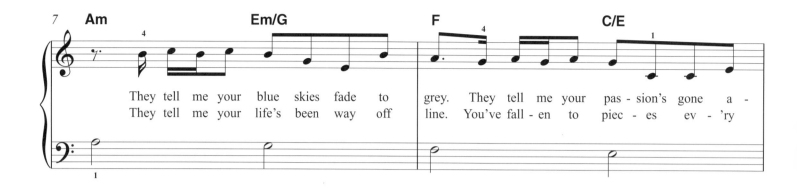

They tell me your blue skies fade to grey. They tell me your pas - sion's gone a -
They tell me your life's been way off line. You've fall - en to piec - es ev - 'ry

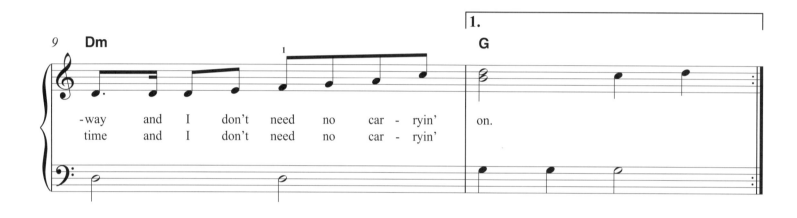

-way and I don't need no car - ryin' on.
time and I don't need no car - ryin'

1.

2.

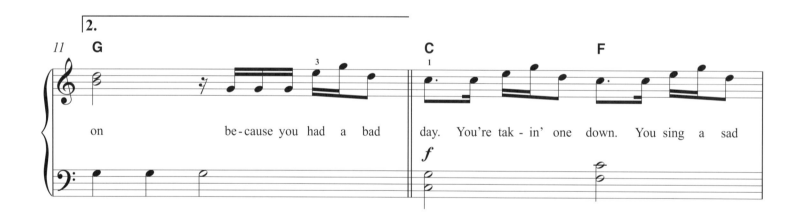

on be - cause you had a bad day. You're tak - in' one down. You sing a sad

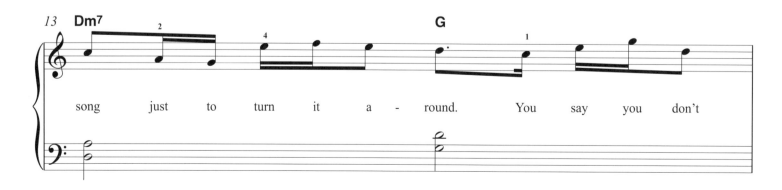

song just to turn it a - round. You say you don't

know. You tell me don't lie. You work at a

smile and you go for a ride. You had a bad day. The cam-'ra don't lie. You're com-in' back

down and you real-ly don't mind. You had a bad day._____ You had a bad

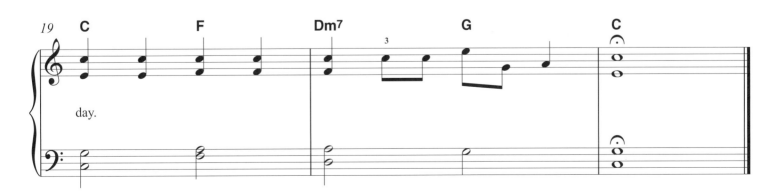

day.

Best Day of My Life

Words and Music by Zachary Barnett, James Adam Shelley, Matthew Sanchez, David Rublin, Shep Goodman and Aaron Accetta

Having sold over a million copies in the USA alone, and featured prominently in adverts for Hyundai plus a major Hollywood movie, 'Best Day Of My Life' has been a major breakthrough for New York band American Authors. The song's video is a feel-good, memorable clip featuring a man hanging around Brooklyn playing basketball, drinking beers and getting a tattoo with his imaginary friend.

Hints & Tips: The fingering of the fast semiquavers/sixteenth notes (e.g. bar 9) may look tricky but alternating between the first and second fingers will help make the notes more even.

Beautiful Day

Words by Bono
Music by U2

The lead single from U2's album, *All That You Can't Leave Behind,* this optimistic anthem, about a man who has lost everything but nevertheless can find joy in what he still has, won three Grammy Awards in 2001 after becoming the veteran Irish rock band's fourth UK No. 1 single since their emergence in the early 1980s.

Hints & Tips: The left hand has a tricky part to play so work it out slowly and rhythmically, carefully placing the first beat of each bar. Keep it moving.

care, the traf - fic is stuck,

and you're not mov - ing____ a - ny - where.

You thought you'd found a friend,___

to take you out of this place.

Some - one you could lend a hand in re -

13

Crazy Little Thing Called Love

Words and Music by Freddie Mercury

Allegedly composed by Freddie Mercury whilst having a bath, in 1980 it became Queen's first No. 1 single in the USA. *The Game*, the album on which it featured, was the first Queen album to be released on CD, their first to reach No. 1 in the US and the first to use synthesizers, as the band adopted the bass-driven grooves of the day.

Hints & Tips: Keep both hands light throughout. Look through the piece carefully before playing to make sure you know where all the accidentals are. Count through bars 33–36, making sure full value is given to the rests in between the triplets.

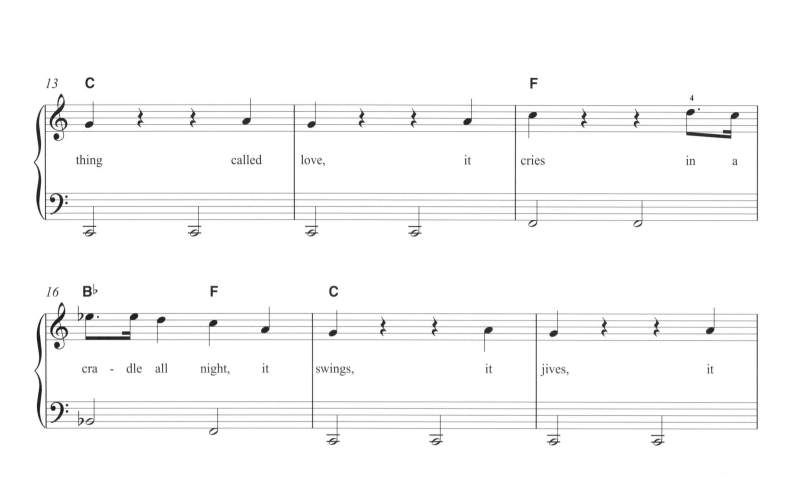

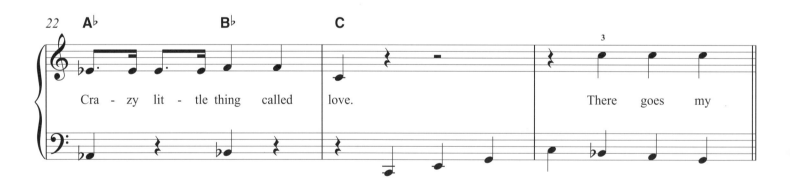

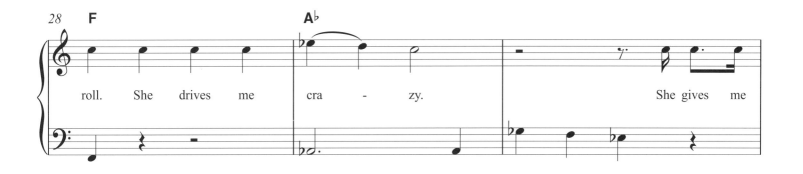

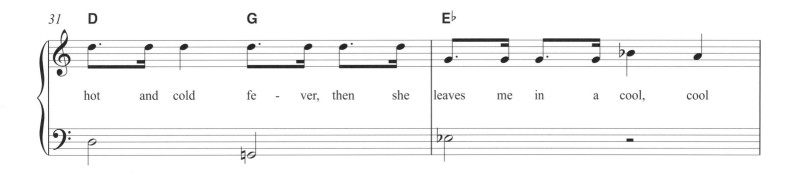

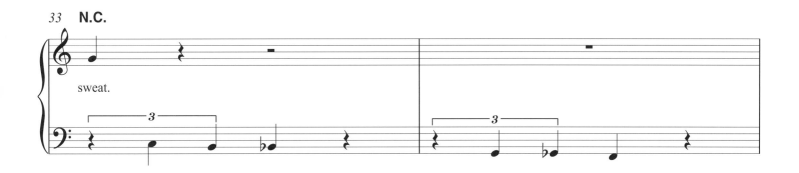

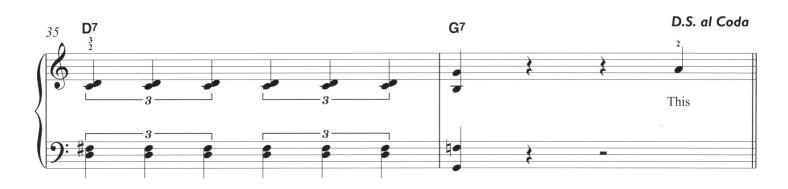

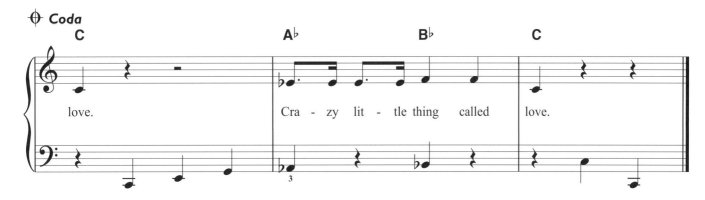

Call Me Maybe

Words and Music by Carly Rae Jepsen, Joshua Ramsay and Tavish Crowe

This songstress appeared on the 2007 series of *Canadian Idol* and won third place. After the *Canadian Idol* concert tour, Jepsen was signed, but it wasn't until 2012 that she released this No. 1 smash hit. It was iTunes' most purchased song in 2012 and resulted in Jepsen being chatted up by men who used her own lyrics to woo her! As her career blossomed, so did an unlikely friendship with actor Tom Hanks, who went on to star in her 2015 music video for 'I Really Like You'.

Hints & Tips: Try a slow tempo at first so you get used to the repeated notes. Practise the left hand on its own in the chorus; try and get both notes to sound exactly together. If this is too tricky just play the bottom note each time.

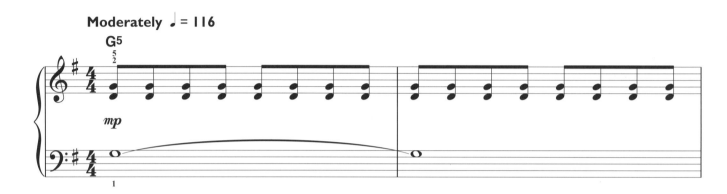

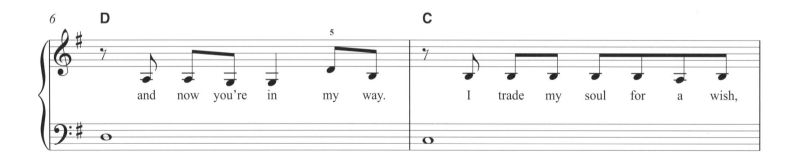

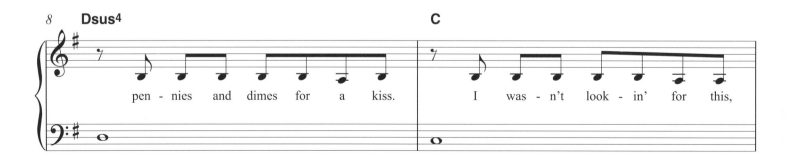

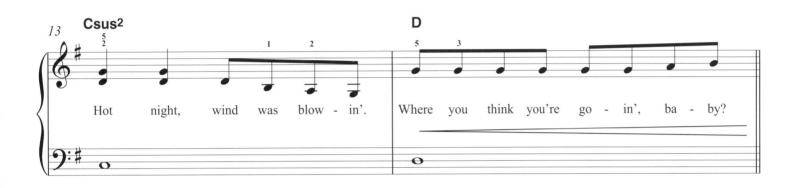

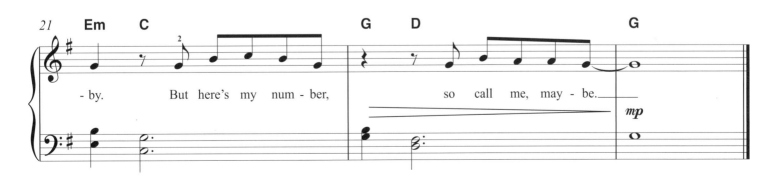

Can't Stop the Feeling!

from TROLLS

Words and Music by Justin Timberlake, Max Martin and Shellback

Justin Timberlake's funky, disco-inspired pop hit was written for the 2016 animated film *Trolls*, for which Timberlake acted as executive music producer. The song marks a return to the charts for the star, putting him back in the US number one spot after nine years.

Hints & Tips: Try practising the left-hand part in the chorus separately to establish a solid disco feel before adding the syncopated melody.

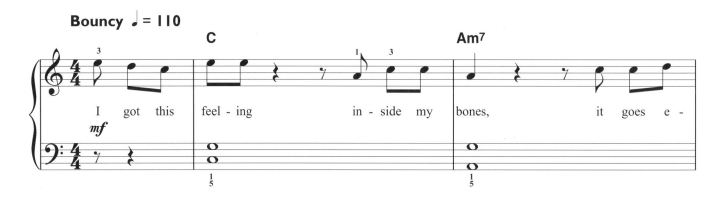

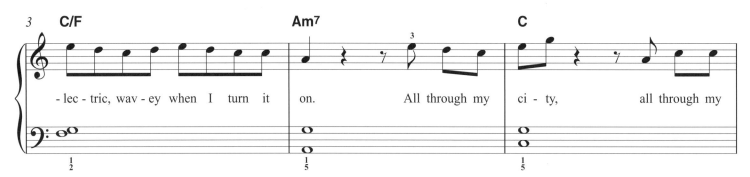

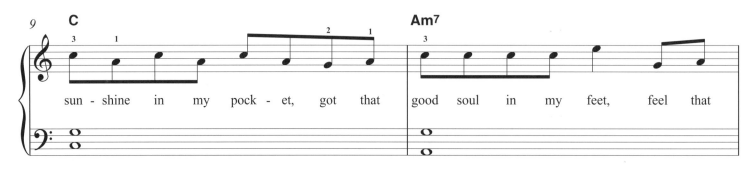

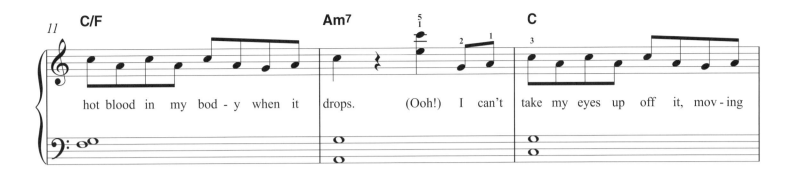

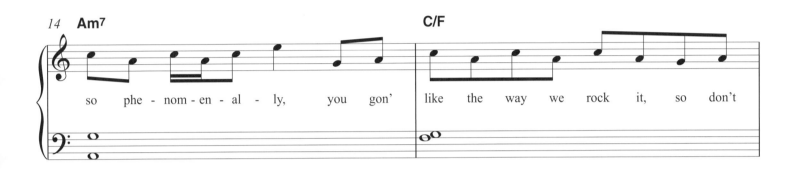

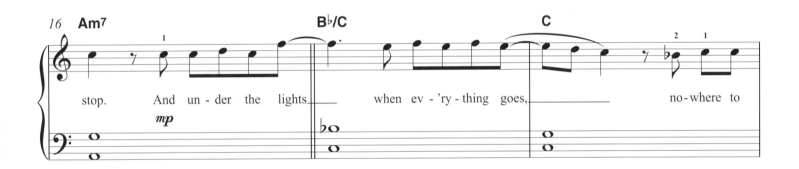

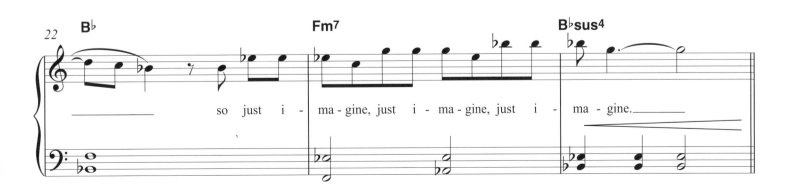

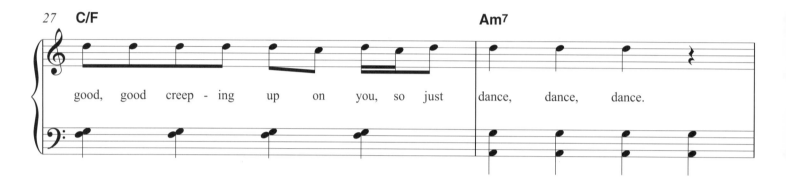

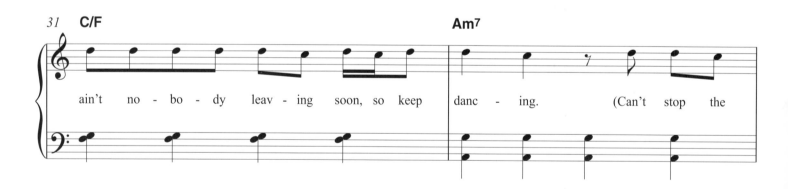

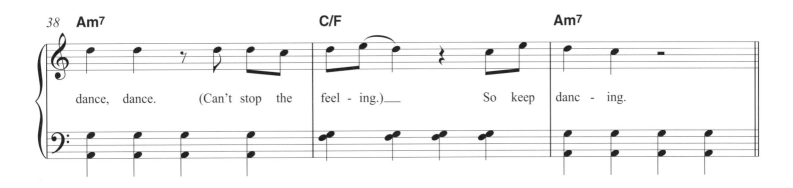

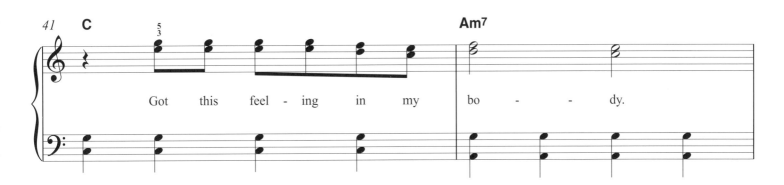

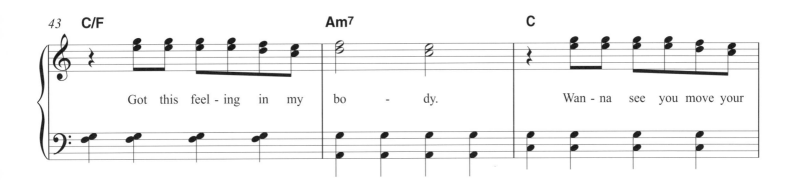

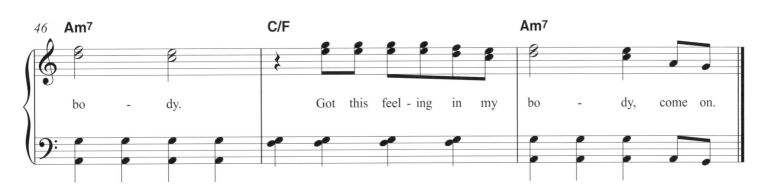

Cups (When I'm Gone)
from the Motion Picture Soundtrack PITCH PERFECT

Words and Music by A.P. Carter, Luisa Gerstein and Heloise Tunstall-Behrens

This song has a history of interpretation preceding the version in *Pitch Perfect* (2012). It was the English act, Lulu and the Lampshades, who started the trend of singing their rendition of the song accompanied by plastic cups on YouTube. Anna Burden soon followed, from whom Anna Kendrick then learned the song for the movie. At just 1m 17s long, it became the second shortest single to feature in the Hot 100, behind the band Womenfolk with their 1m 2s hit, 'Little Boxes'.

Hints & Tips: Be careful with the fast tempo marking in this one. Try it slower if you struggle with the rhythm. The left hand plays 5ths almost throughout the chorus. Set your hand into a fixed position.

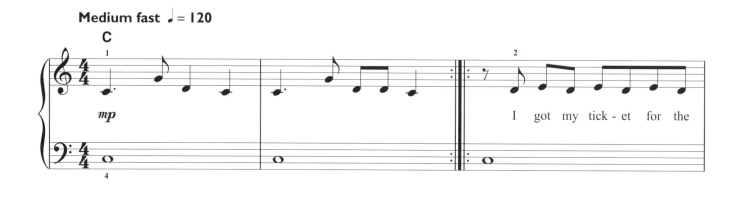

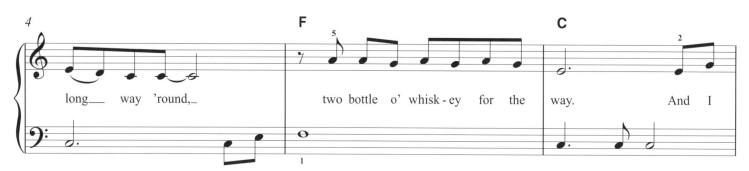

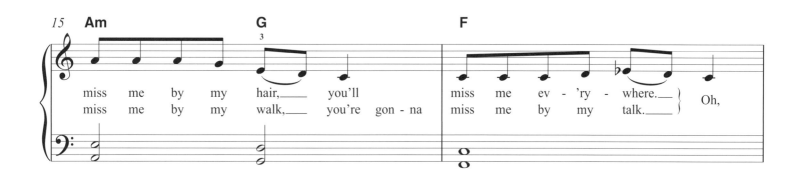

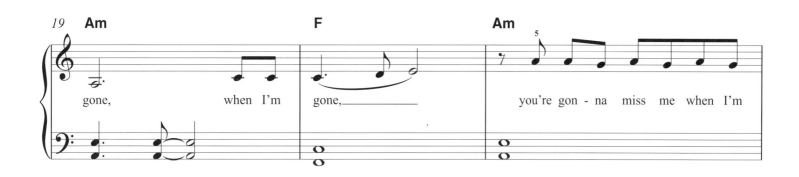

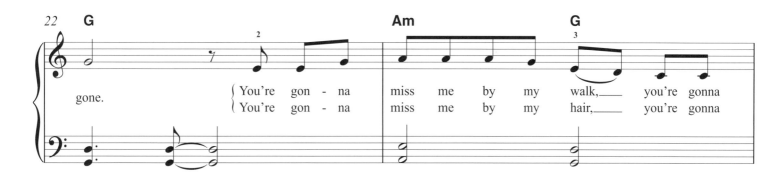

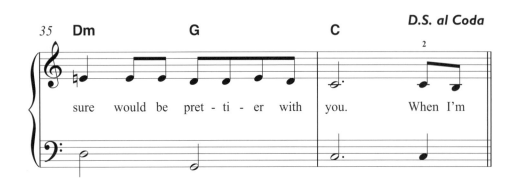

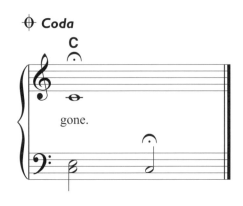

Don't Start Now

Words and Music by Dua Lipa, Caroline Ailin, Ian Kirkpatrick and Emily Schwartz

This track comes from Dua Lipa's second album, *Future Nostalgia*, released in 2020. The release of the album at the beginning of a new decade prompted Lipa to state that she was launching into "a new era with a new sound". This upbeat song is full of positivity after a breakup, warning her ex-lover not to turn up to the party because she'll be dancing with someone else! During the Covid-19 pandemic, the lyrics 'don't show up, don't come out' were used on social media as a tongue-in-cheek reference to the new social distancing regulations that forbid public meetings at the time.

Hints & Tips: Here the left hand illustrates the two distinct moods: static long notes and driving crotchets/quarter notes; try and feel the dance beat. Take care with the octave stretch in the right hand.

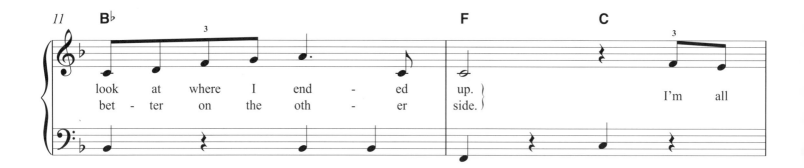

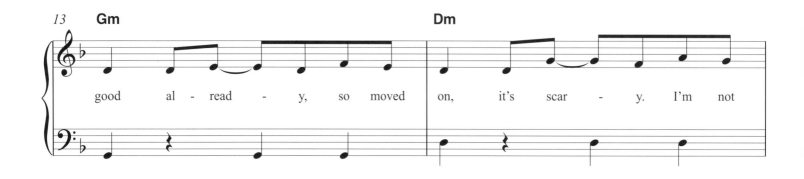

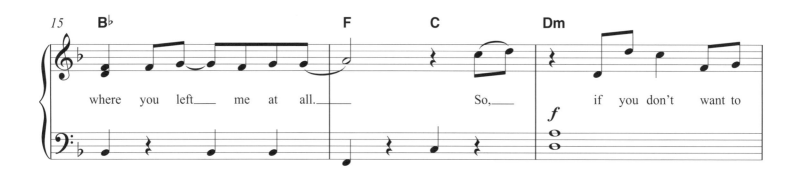

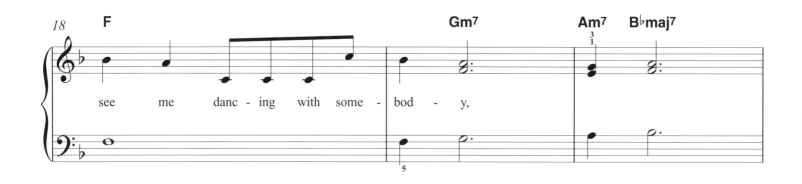

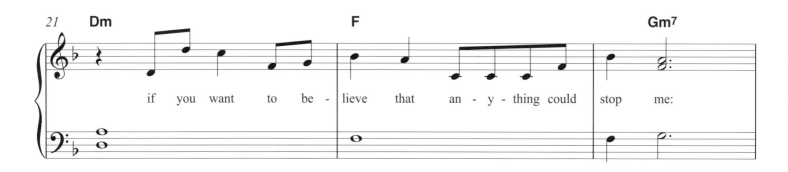

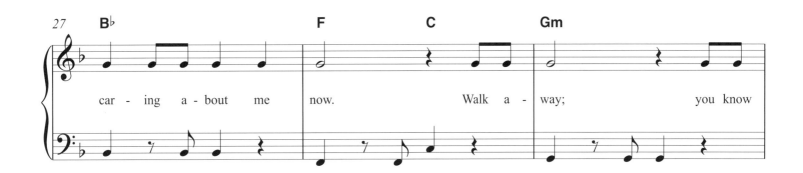

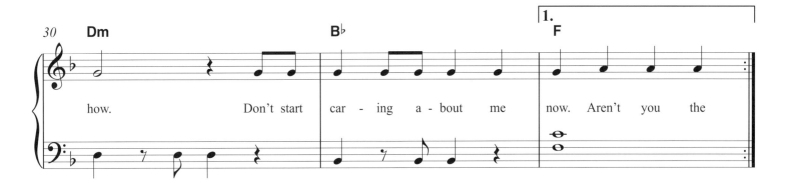

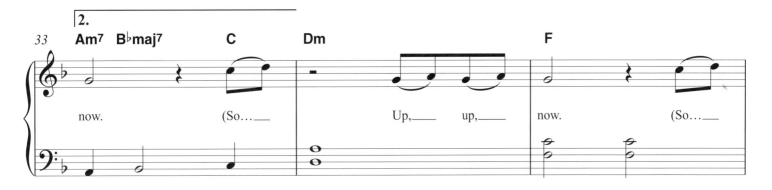

Fight Song

Words and Music by Rachel Platten and Dave Bassett

Just as Rachel Platten was about to give up her 12-year-long career as a musician, she wrote 'Fight Song' as her own personal anthem to keep going. After Columbia Records heard the song in 2014, they signed her and re-released the single in 2015, when it reached No. 1 in the UK. The music-recognising app, Shazam, also played a part in getting Platten signed, as it was used many times by listeners hoping to find out the name of the artist upon hearing the uplifting track.

Hints & Tips: The verse of this song should be very gentle. It gradually builds up until you get to the chorus, which can be much louder. Remember that the right hand is written in the bass clef on the third and fourth pages.

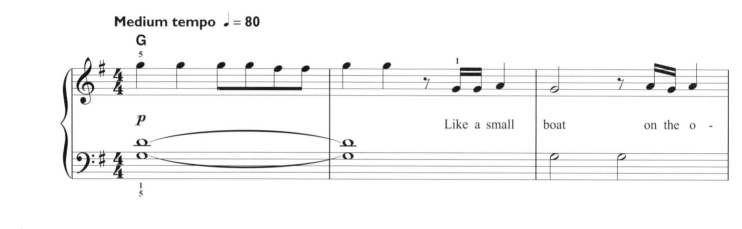

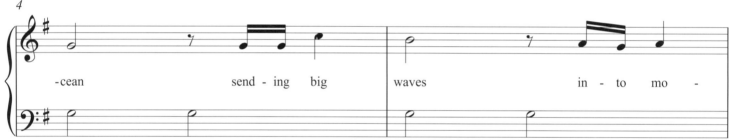

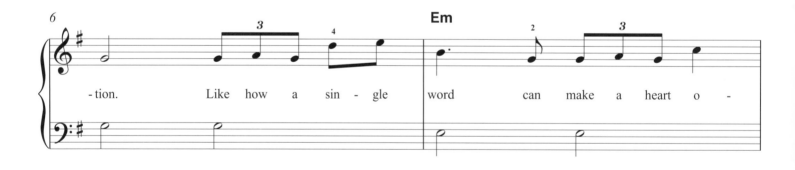

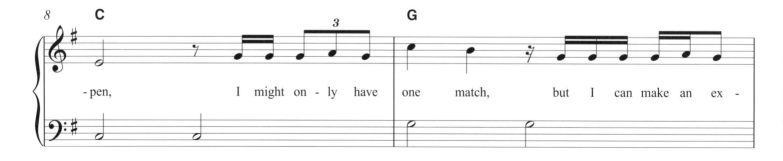

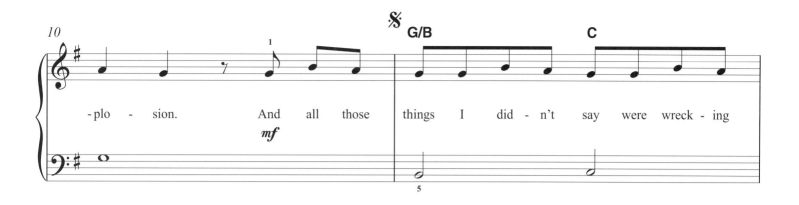

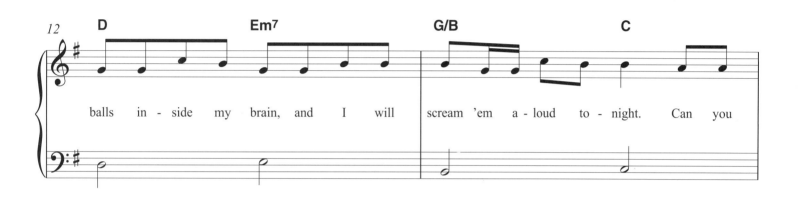

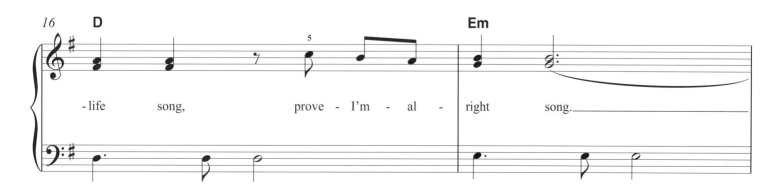

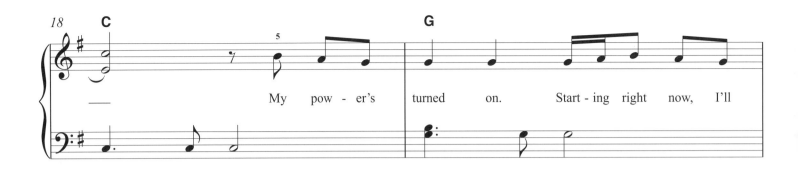

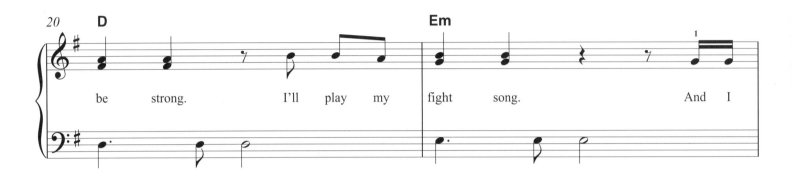

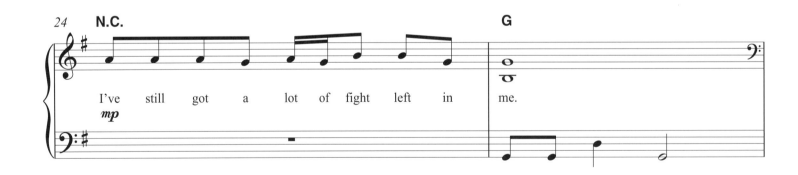

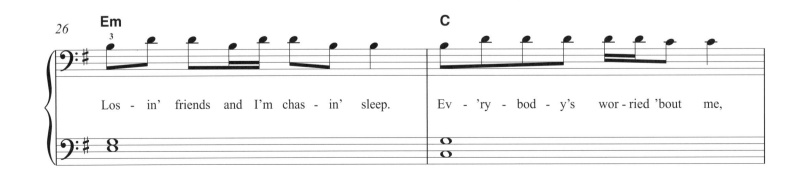

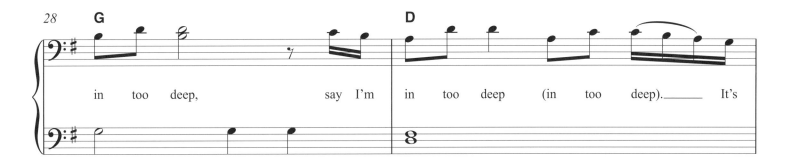

in too deep, say I'm in too deep (in too deep). It's

been two years. I miss my home, but there's a fire burn - in' in my bones. I

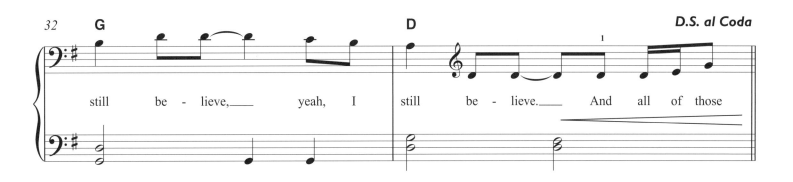

D.S. al Coda

still be - lieve, yeah, I still be - lieve. And all of those

Coda

I've still got a lot of fight left in me. No,

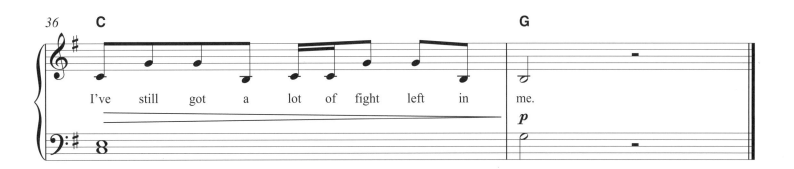

I've still got a lot of fight left in me.

p

Firework

Words and Music by Katy Perry, Mikkel Eriksen, Tor Erik Hermansen, Esther Dean and Sandy Wilhelm

Written as anthem for self-empowerment, 'Firework' was considered by Katy Perry to be the most important song on her album *Teenage Dream*. The single reached No. 1 on the US singles chart, becoming her third US chart topper from the album – her fourth US No. 1 in total. This feat made Perry the first female artist since Madonna to achieve three consecutive number one singles from the same album.

Hints & Tips: The repeated quavers/eighth notes in the left hand could sound quite heavy if you're not careful, so keep them bouncy.

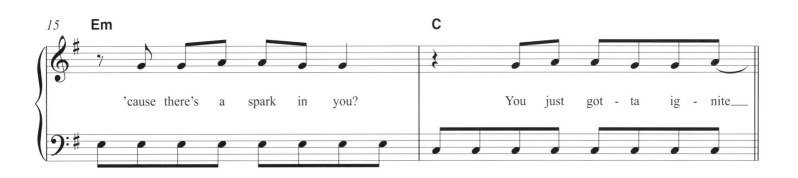

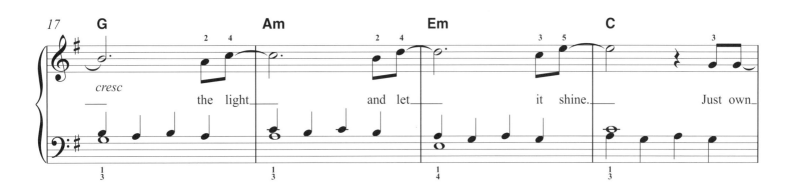

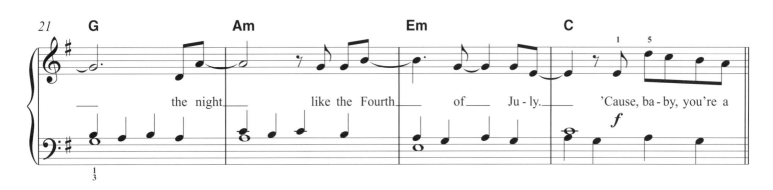

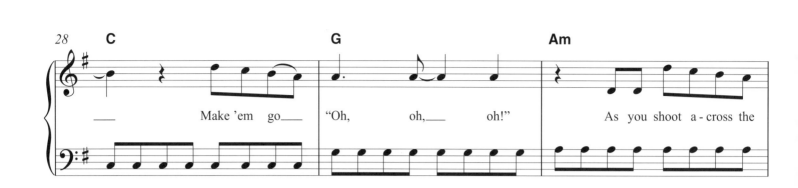

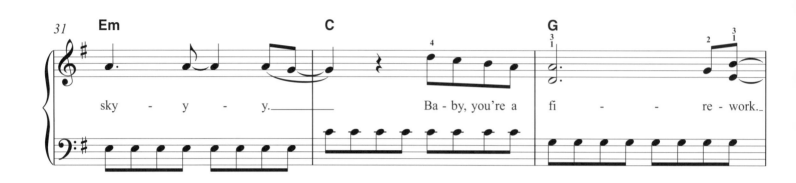

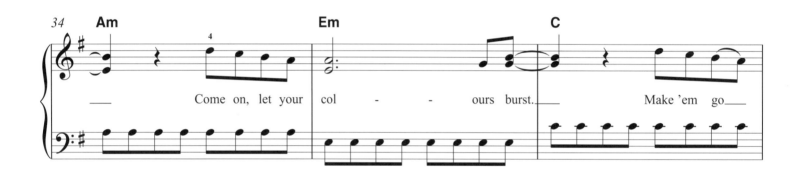

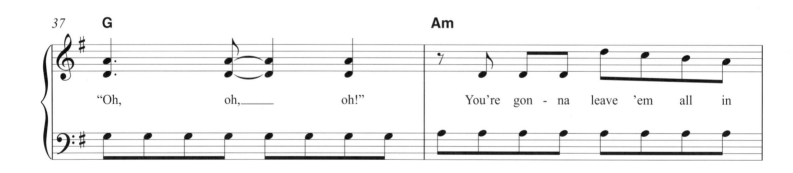

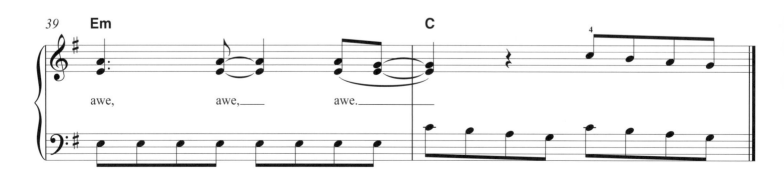

Hakuna Matata
from THE LION KING

Music by Elton John
Lyrics by Tim Rice

The title of this song, one of three from Disney movie *The Lion King* to be nominated in 1995 for an Academy Award®, is a Swahili phrase which means 'no worries' or 'no problem'. It is sung by Timon, a meerkat, and Pumbaa, a warthog, as they try to convince the lion cub Simba to forget his troubled past.

Hints & Tips: The opening to this song is like a recitative, a style of speech-like singing, usually found in operas between songs, telling the story, and not always particularly rhythmic.

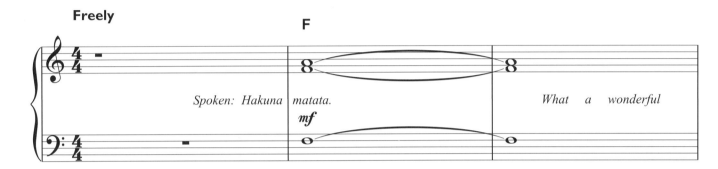

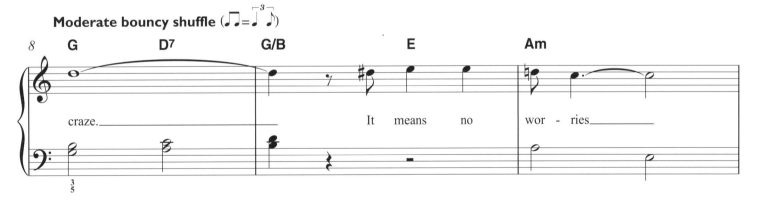

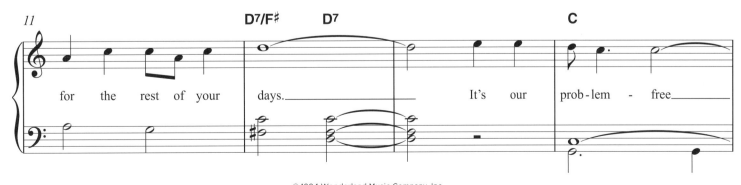

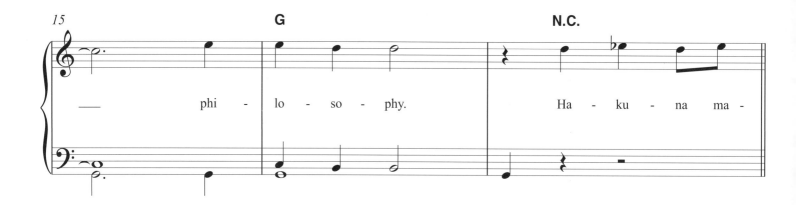

phi - lo - so - phy. Ha - ku - na ma -

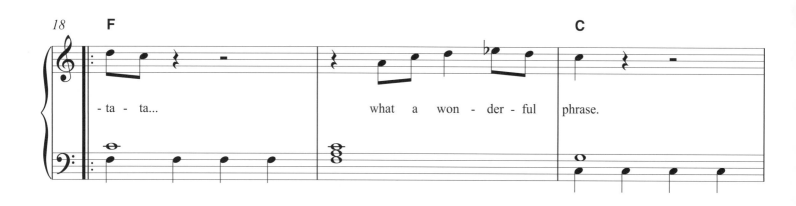

- ta - ta... what a won - der - ful phrase.

Ha - ku - na ma - ta - ta... ain't no pass - ing

craze. It means no wor - ries

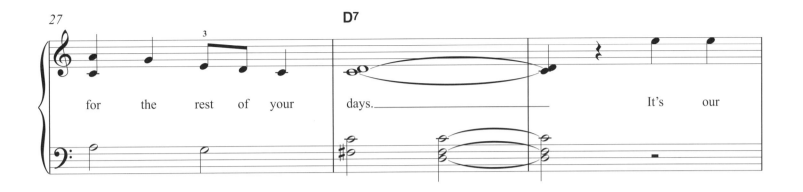

for the rest of your days._____ It's our

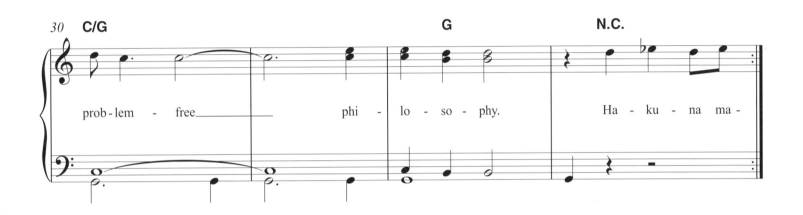

prob-lem - free_____ phi - lo - so - phy. Ha - ku - na ma-

- ta - ta... Ha - ku - na ma - ta - ta... Ha - ku - na ma-

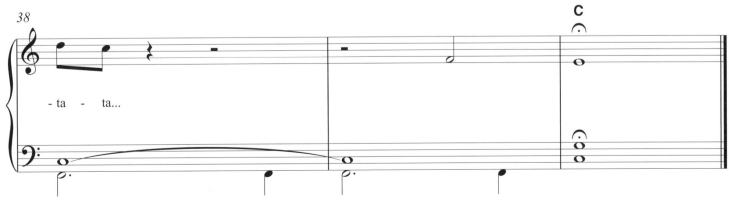

- ta - ta...

Happy
from DESPICABLE ME 2

Words and Music by Pharrell Williams

The most successful song from *Despicable Me 2*, 'Happy' was used to promote the soundtrack to the film.
Not only was it one of the biggest hits of 2013 and early 2014, but the song is also able to boast the world's first
ever 24-hour music video, featuring various performers and celebrities dancing along to the track in four minute loops.

**Hints & Tips: The left hand plays an important role all through this song, so make sure you bring it out
whenever it has a solo, e.g. bars 4 and 5. It also plays the backing melody at the chorus, starting in bar 17.**

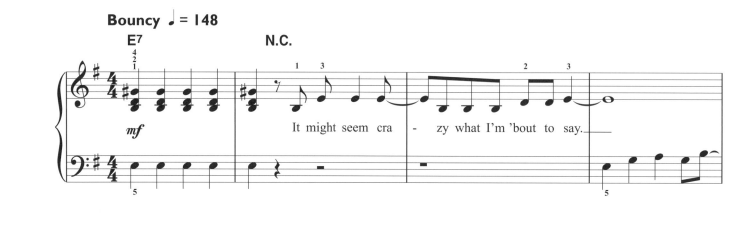

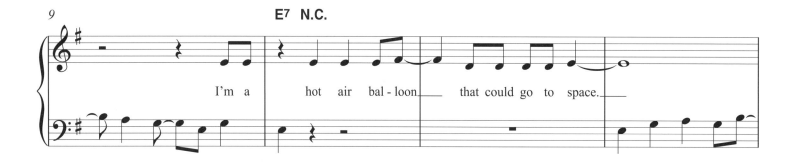

Havana

Words and Music by Camila Cabello, Louis Bell, Pharrell Williams, Adam Feeney, Ali Tamposi,
Jeffery Lamar Williams, Brian Lee, Andrew Wotman, Brittany Hazzard and Kaan Gunesberk

Even before the official break was announced for girl group Fifth Harmony in 2018, ex-member Camila Cabello
was already making No. 1 hits as a solo artist! 'Havana' was a chart-topper for the vocalist in 2017, co-written
with Pharrell Williams about the capital of her home country, Cuba. The music video won Video of the Year
at the 2018 MTV Awards, the same year that Cabello herself won Artist of the Year.

Hints & Tips: The left-hand dotted rhythm in the intro helps convey the Latin feel of this song.
Be careful not to play this too fast — you have a lot of triplets (three notes per beat) on the second page.

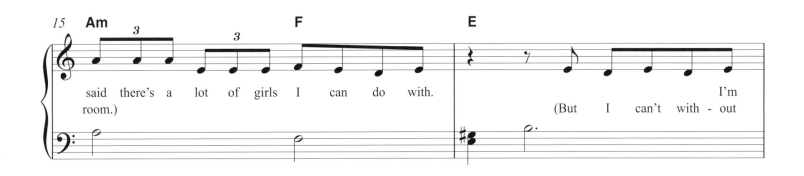

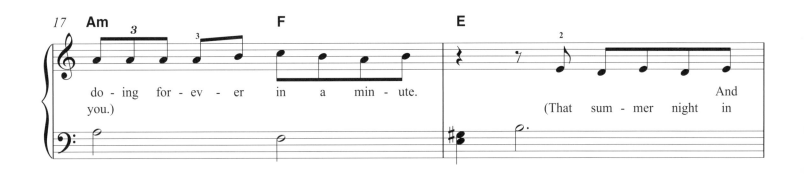

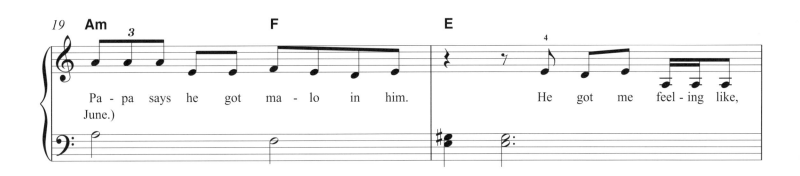

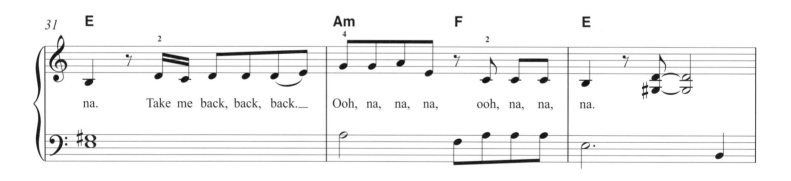

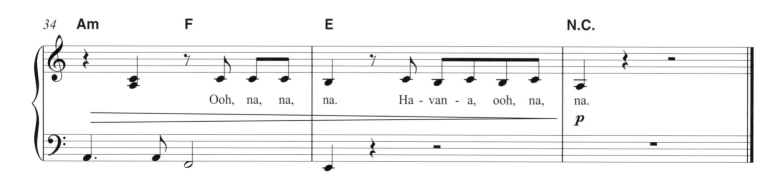

High Hopes

Words and Music by Brendon Urie, Samuel Hollander, William Lobban Bean, Jonas Jeberg, Jacob Sinclair, Jenny Owen Youngs, Ilsey Juber, Lauren Pritchard and Tayla Parx

By the time of this release, Panic! At The Disco had gone from four members to just one, with only frontman Brendon Urie left. In this song from the 2018 album, *Pray for the Wicked*, Urie wanted to sing about his dream of playing on stage as a child and the triumph over adversity as he continues to pursue his music career. Urie has also appeared on soundtracks for major films *The Greatest Showman* (2017) with 'The Greatest Show' and *Frozen 2* (2019) with 'Into The Unknown'.

Hints & Tips: The intro is almost like a fanfare. Remember the B♭ in the key signature.
The left-hand minims/half notes drive the music forward.

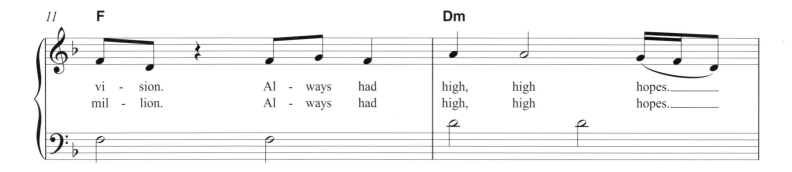

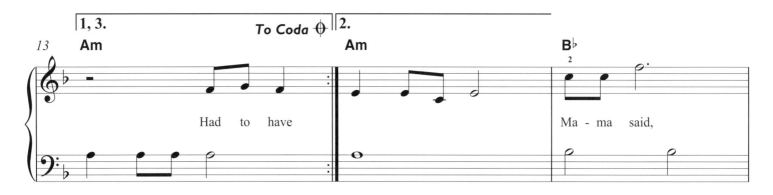

Re - write your his - to - ry. Light up your wild - est dreams.' Mu - se - um vic - to - ries,

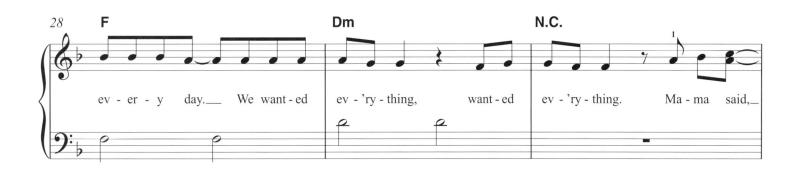

ev - er - y day.__ We want - ed ev - 'ry - thing, want - ed ev - 'ry - thing. Ma - ma said,__

__ 'Don't give up.__ It's a lit - tle com - pli - cat -

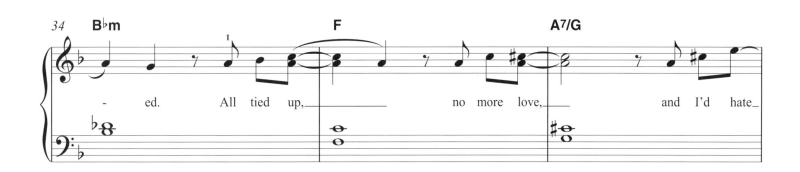

- ed. All tied up,__ no more love,__ and I'd hate__

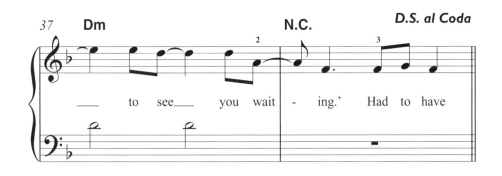

__ to see__ you wait - ing.' Had to have

Let It Go
from FROZEN

Music and Lyrics by Kristen Anderson-Lopez and Robert Lopez

'Let It Go' has since become one of the best-selling singles of all time and has earnt many accolades, including the Academy Award® for Best Original Song at the 86th Academy Awards. Composed by husband and wife songwriters Kristen Anderson-Lopez and Robert Lopez, the song was written for and originally performed by Idina Menzel, who's powerful vocals perfectly voiced Elsa's newfound freedom in the film. The song was reportedly composed in just a single day, after an inspiring walk in New York's Prospect Park.

Hints & Tips: There's a lot to watch out for in this, so look through and mark in pencil anything you're unsure of. Practise these bits thoroughly first before putting the whole piece together.

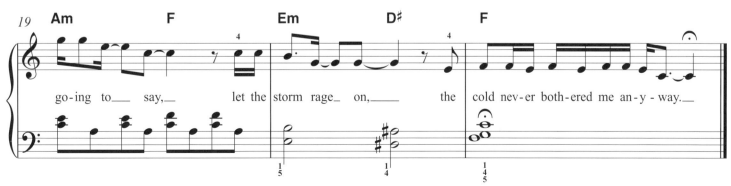

49

I Love Rock 'n Roll

Words and Music by Alan Merrill and Jake Hooker

This song was originally written and recorded by British band The Arrows in 1975. Joan Jett wanted to cover it while she was part of the girl group The Runaways but the rest of the band weren't keen on the song. Eventually, she recorded it first in 1979, but the version we know and love was recorded in 1981 with her band The Blackhearts. The song was also used in the 2002 movie, *Crossroads*, starring Britney Spears, who sings a version of the track as her character, Lucy.

Hints & Tips: You need to count carefully in this song as there are long stretches of rests. There is also a 2/4 bar at the end of the chorus. Practise bar 4 with just the right hand first and make sure you're reading both flats correctly.

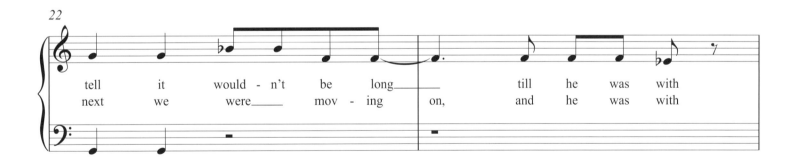

I'm a Believer

Words and Music by Neil Diamond

This song was written by Neil Diamond, who gave it to The Monkees to record and release in 1966. The track hit the No. 1 spot in the US, before Diamond recorded his own version in 1967 for his album, *Just for You*. Over thirty years later, Smash Mouth created their version of the song for the movie soundtrack to the 2001 film, *Shrek,* which also featured their popular hit, 'All Star'. You can hear Eddie Murphy singing 'I'm a Believer' in the film as his character, the beloved Donkey.

Hints & Tips: This song is in D major — F♯ and C♯ in the key signature. Choose a tempo that enables you to play the well known left-hand (guitar) riff evenly. Also watch out for dotted rhythms.

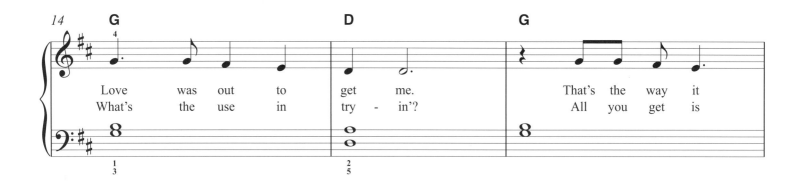

Love   was   out   to   get   me.   That's the way   it
What's the use in   try - in'?   All   you get   is

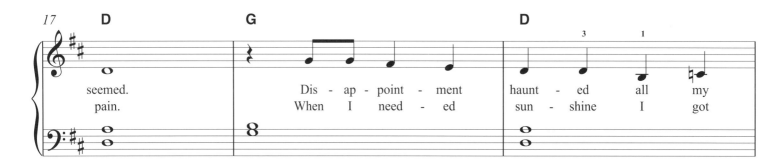

seemed.   Dis - ap - point - ment   haunt - ed   all   my
pain.   When I need - ed   sun - shine I   got

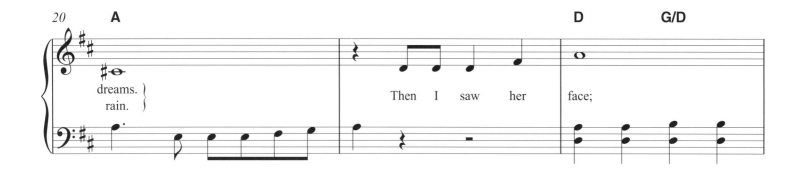

dreams. }
rain. }   Then I saw her   face;

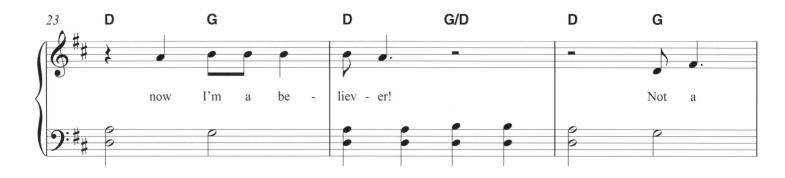

now I'm a be - liev - er!   Not a

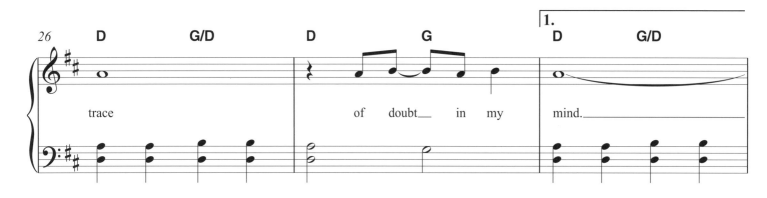

1.

trace   of doubt in my   mind.

Into the Unknown
from FROZEN 2

Music and Lyrics by Kristen Anderson-Lopez and Robert Lopez

We follow Elsa's footsteps to discover more about her powers in *Frozen 2*, with 'Into the Unknown'
playing a central role in the movie's storyline. Questioning the meaning of her 'secret siren',
Elsa sings this tune to the disembodied voice that keeps her awake, luring her to follow its call.
It's another epic journey for Elsa in this second film, accompanied by Anna, Kristoff, Sven and Olaf.

Hints & tips: Try to feel the dotted crotchet/quarter note pulse of this song. The left hand really drives the song
forward from bar 33, then the music goes back into its shell towards the end, with an echo of the beginning.

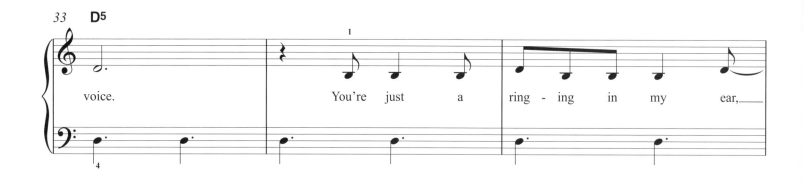

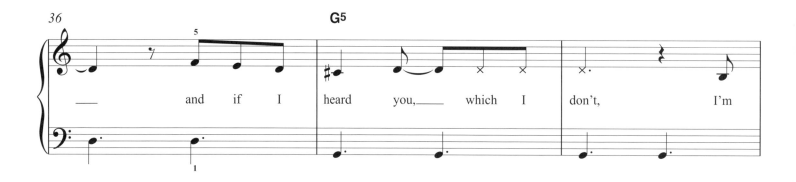

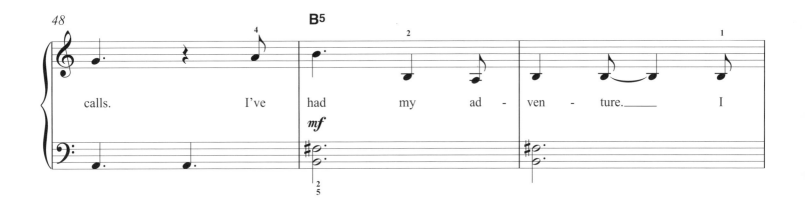

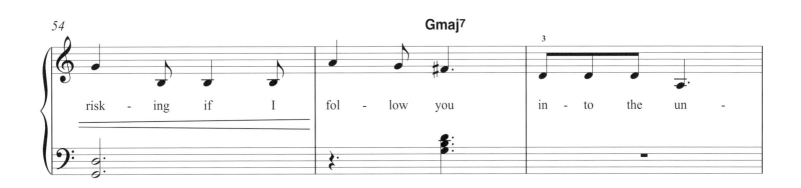

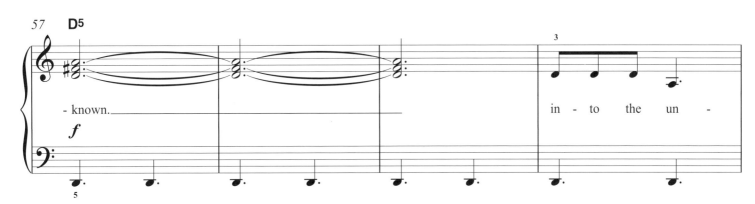

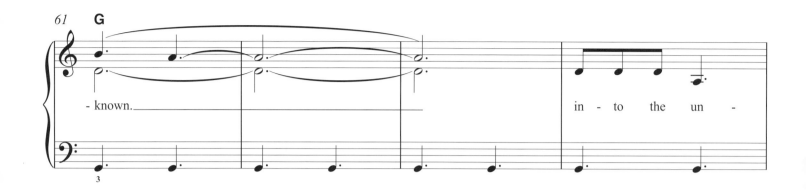

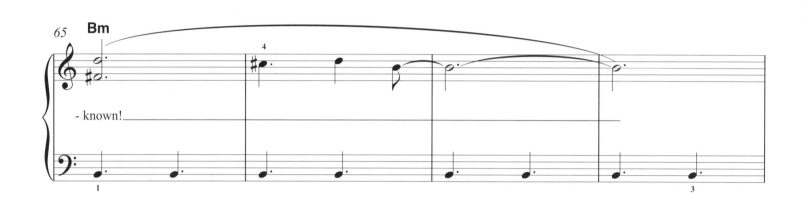

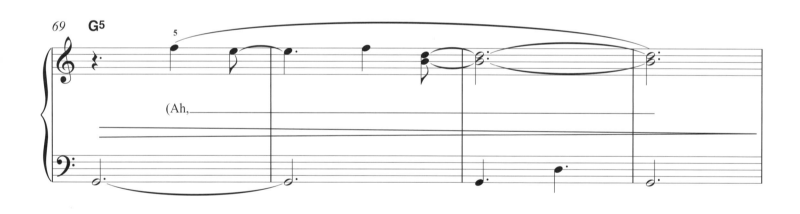

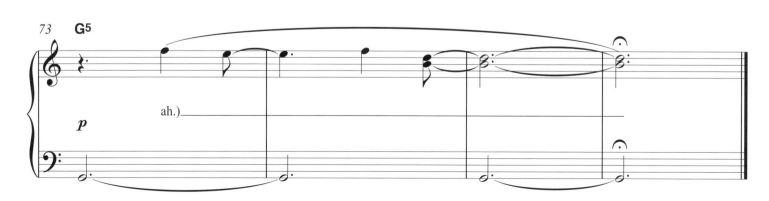

ME!

Words and Music by Taylor Swift, Joel Little and Brendon Urie

This single is from Taylor Swift's 2019 album, *Lover*, and is an empowering number that celebrates individuality. Swift had wanted to collaborate with Panic! At The Disco singer, Brendon Urie, for a long time and felt this was the right track to feature him on. She sent him a message while he was on tour and one month later they were in the studio together. Swift's *Lover* album was a fresh, positive reaffirmation of strength after the 2017 release of her much darker record, *Reputation*.

Hints & Tips: The tempo is fairly quick here, so take it slower if you need to. Take note of the dynamic markings leading into the chorus to really make the most of the melody.

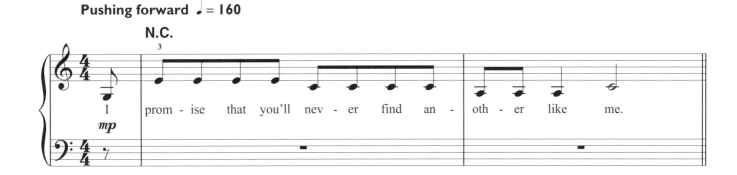

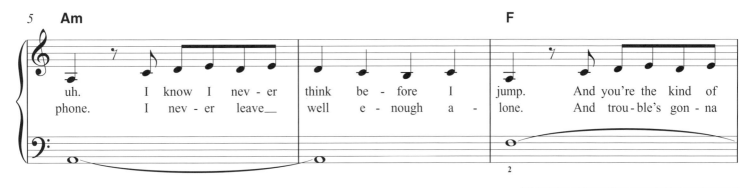

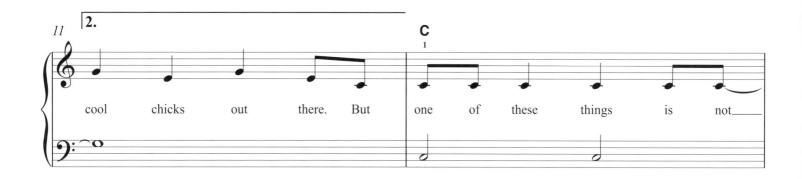

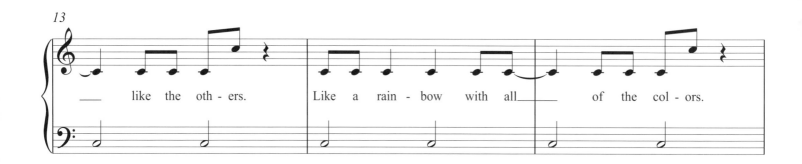

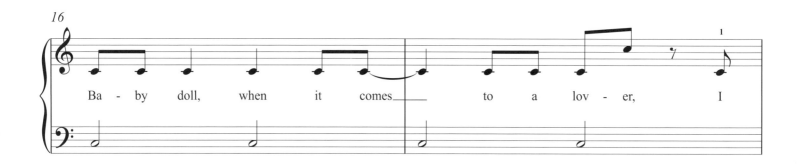

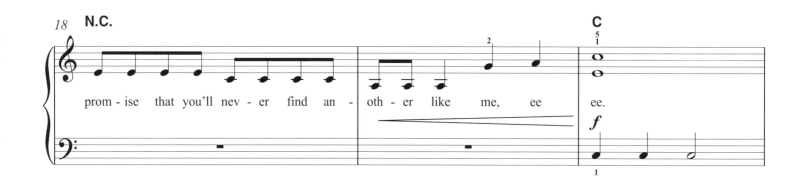

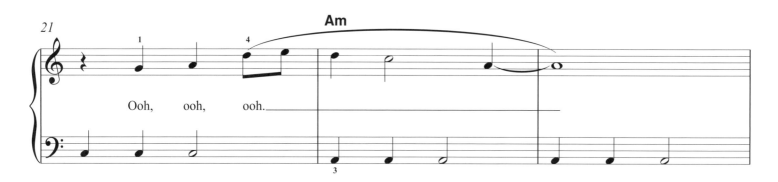

Old Town Road
(Remix)

Words and Music by Trent Reznor, Billy Ray Cyrus,
Jocelyn Donald, Atticus Ross, Kiowa Roukema and Montero Lamar Hill

Lil Nas X gives up his materialistic life to be a cowboy with the help of Miley Cyrus's old man, Billy Ray Cyrus.
Originally, Lil Nas X self-released this track on YouTube before finding himself in the middle of a bidding war
with a number of different labels. Columbia Records were victorious and signed him to their roster in 2019.

Hints & Tips: This song rolls on in a very steady and relaxed tempo.
Keep the right-hand quavers/eighth notes even, and make sure they don't sound too busy.

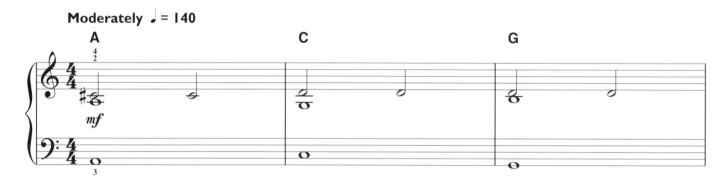

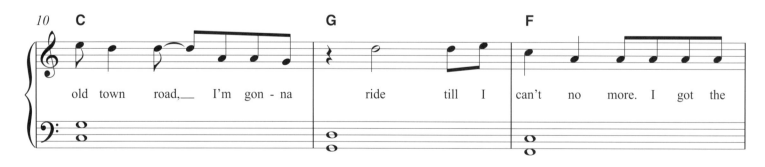

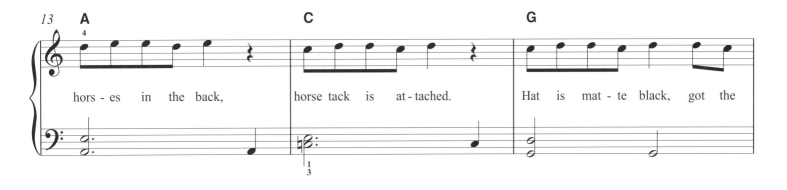

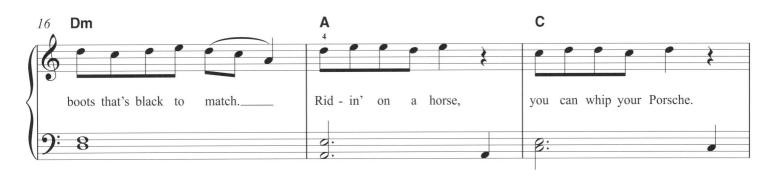

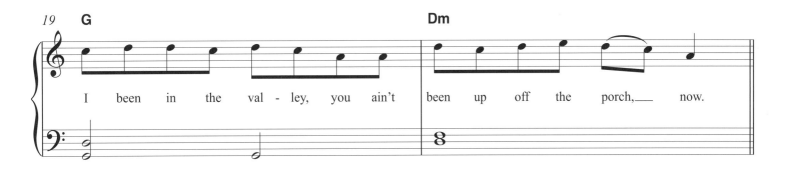

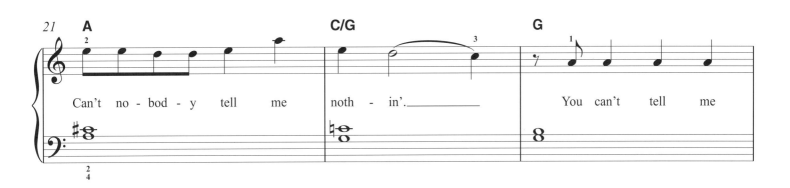

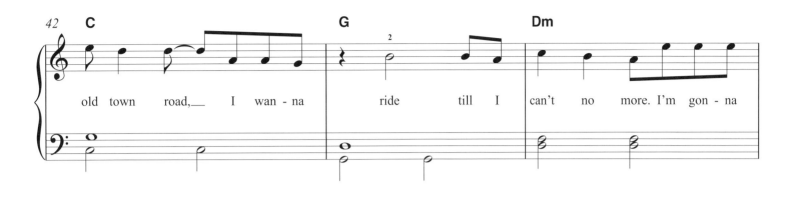

old town road,___ I wan - na ride till I can't no more. I'm gon - na

take my horse to the old town road.___ I'm gon - na ride till I

can't no more. I'm gon - na take my horse to the old town road,___ I'm gon - na

ride till I can't no more.___

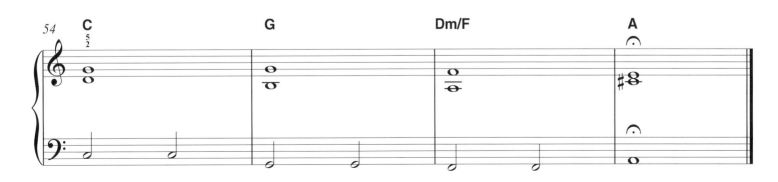

One Call Away

**Words and Music by Charlie Puth, Justin Franks, Breyan Isaac,
Matt Prime, Blake Anthony Carter and Maureen McDonald**

The young singer Charlie Puth wrote this song after speaking to a friend who was lamenting his
long-distance relationship. The piano-based tune delivers the message that, no matter how
geographically far away from you somebody may be, all you have to do is pick up the phone.

Hints & Tips: Use the steady minims/half notes in the left hand to help place the trickier right-hand rhythms.

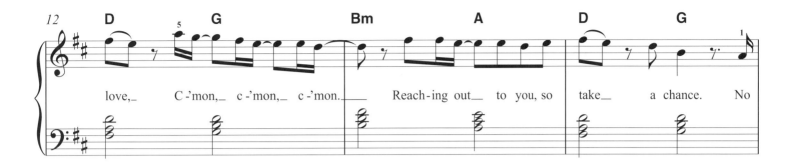

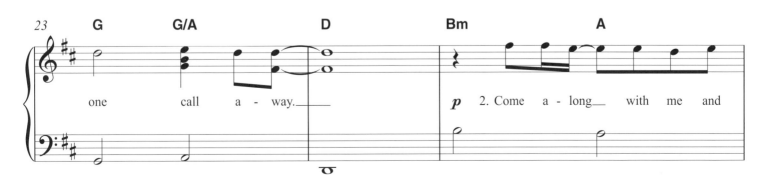

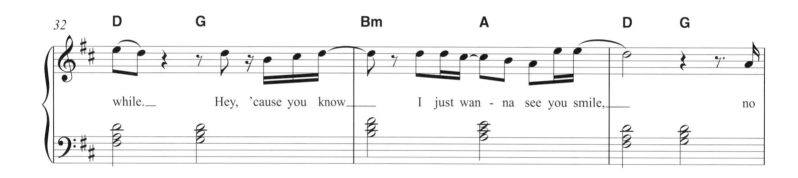

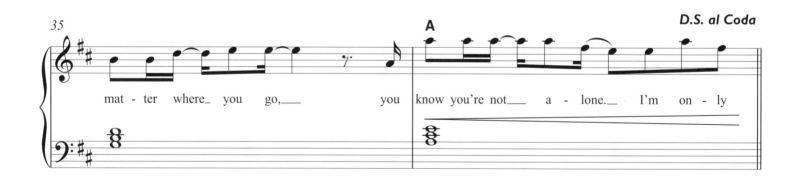

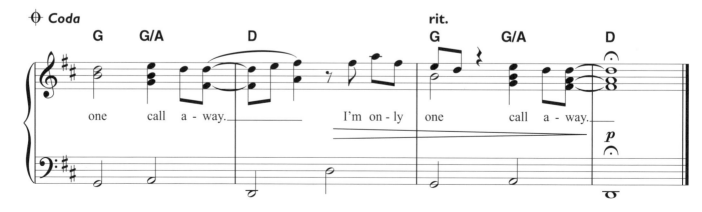

Party in the U.S.A.

Words and Music by Jessica Cornish, Lukasz Gottwald and Claude Kelly

This song apparently paid Jessie J's rent for three years! Originally, the singer and co-writer of 'Party in the USA'
was going to record it herself, but handed the track over to Miley, who included it in her 2009 EP, *Time of Our Lives*.
Miley comes from a very musical family — her dad is Billy Ray Cyrus, famous for his song 'Achy Breaky Heart'
and her godmother is none other than superstar country singer, Dolly Parton!

Hints & Tips: The left hand has a fixed hand position throughout this song. This makes it easier for you to concentrate
on the tricky right hand. There is a wide range of notes in the right hand — make sure you learn the correct fingering.

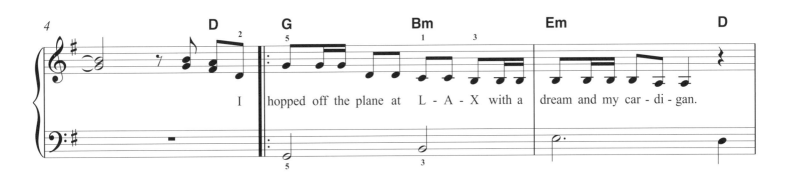

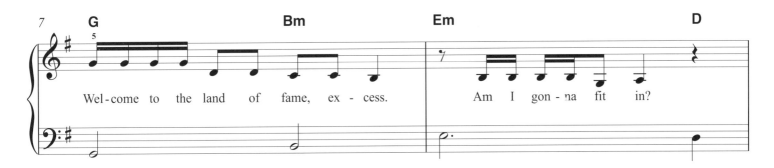

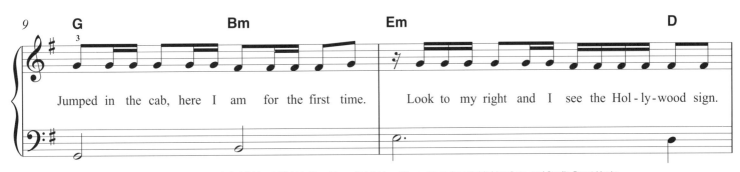

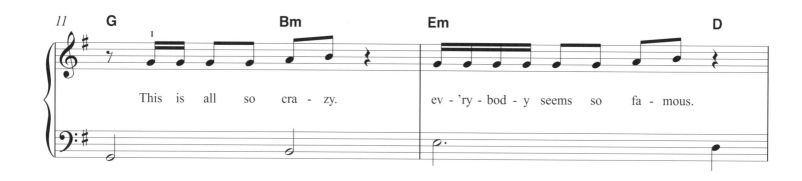

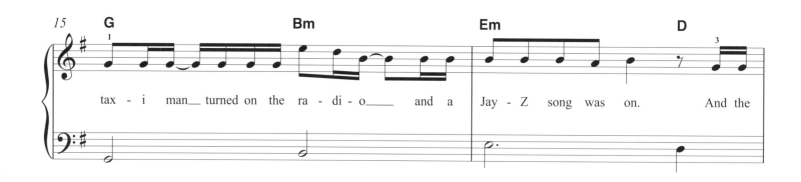

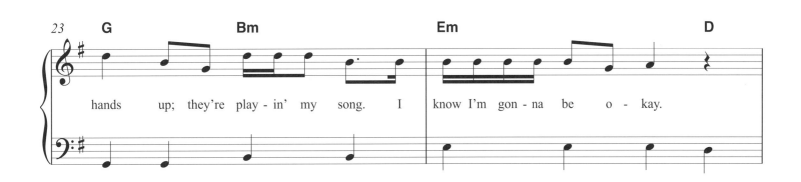

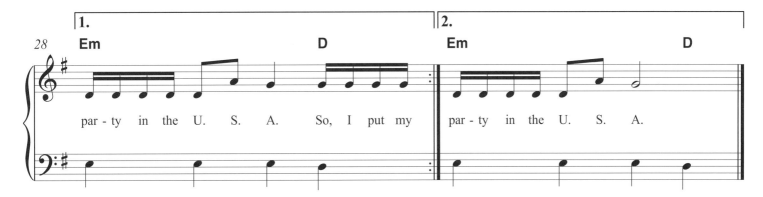

Perfect

Words and Music by Ed Sheeran

Sheeran ended up releasing not one, not two, but three versions of this song! The first was his original release, co-written with folk singer, Amy Wadge, before he set out to create a duet version with 'Queen B' Beyoncé, renaming the song 'Perfect Duet', which earned them the No. 1 spot in the USA. Sheeran also recorded a version with classical singer, Andrea Bocelli, and commissioned his brother, Matthew Sheeran, to write the string arrangement for it. Phew!

Hints & Tips: Take note of the compound triple metre — the song should have a lilting feel to it. Keep a steady pulse in the left hand to help you place the quavers/eighth notes in the right hand.

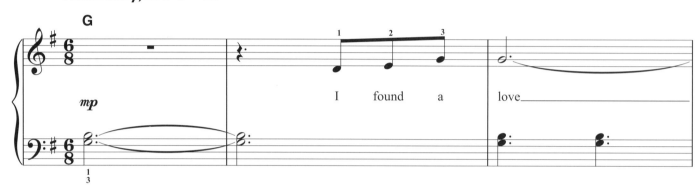

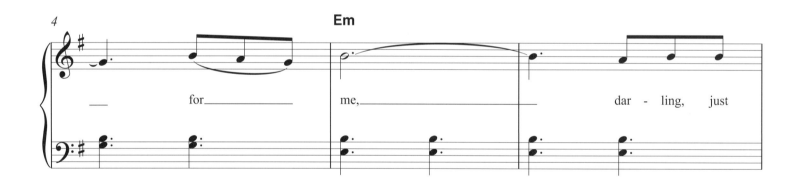

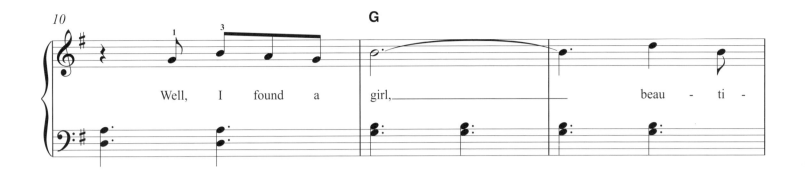

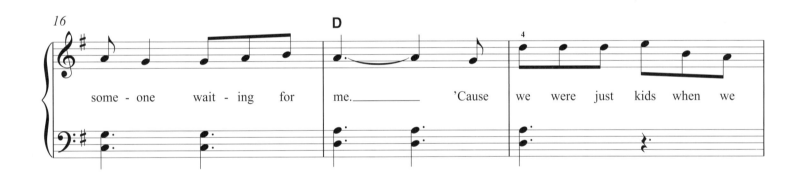

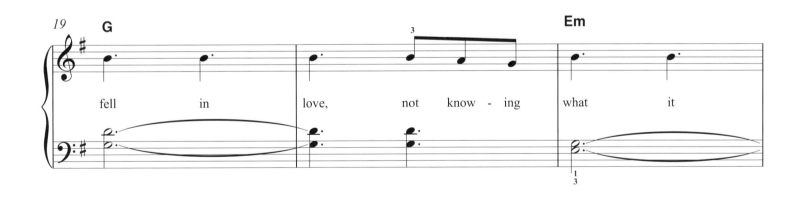

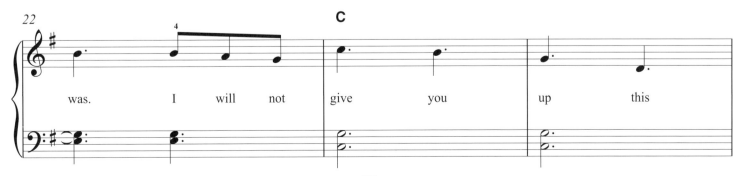

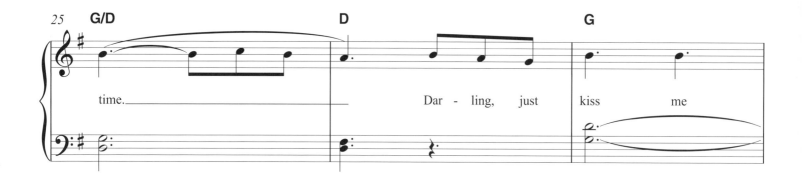

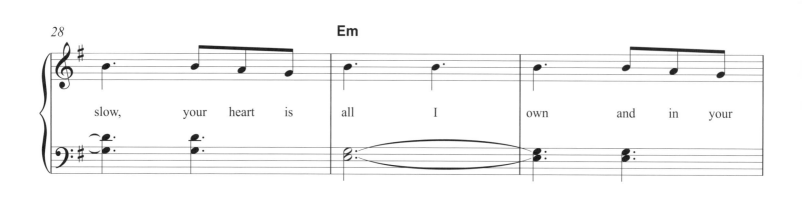

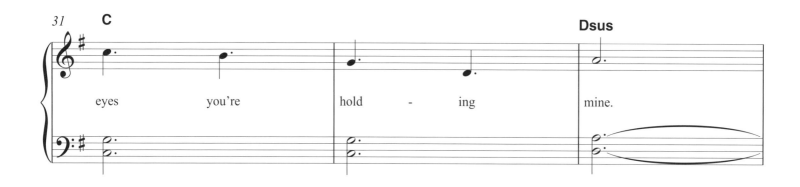

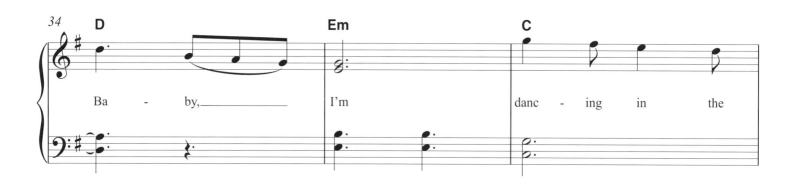

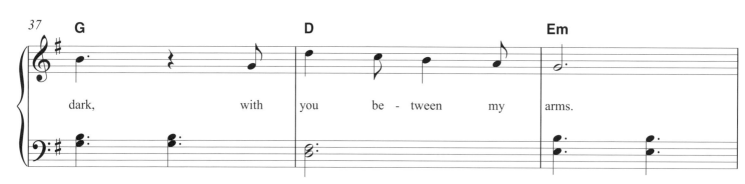

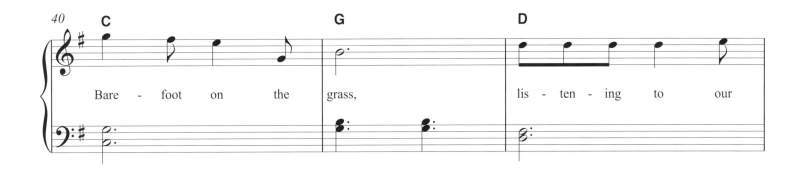

Bare - foot on the grass, lis - ten - ing to our

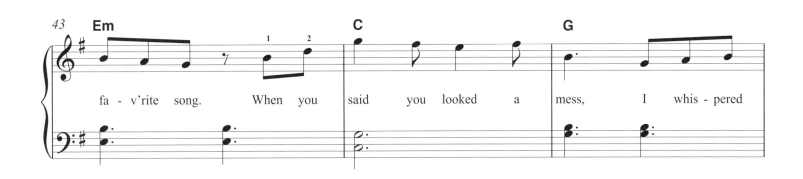

fa - v'rite song. When you said you looked a mess, I whis - pered

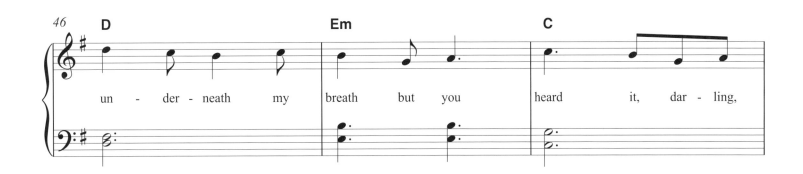

un - der - neath my breath but you heard it, dar - ling,

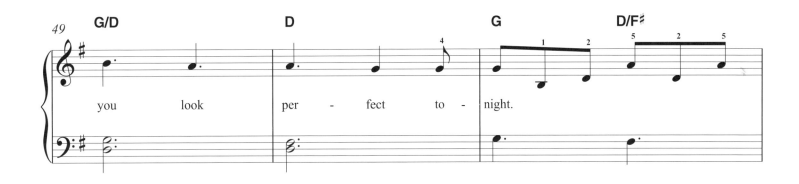

you look per - fect to - night.

Pompeii

Words and Music by Dan Smith

Released as a digital download in February 2013, Bastille's 'Pompeii' peaked at No. 1 in the Irish singles chart for two consecutive weeks and No. 2 in the UK. In Italy it was certified Platinum by the Federation of the Italian Music Industry and broke the record for the longest time spent at top of the UK's Official Streaming Chart.

Hints & Tips: Be careful not to start this one off too fast, otherwise the quavers/eighth notes on the last page will become very tricky to play! Make sure left hand is smooth whenever it's playing two notes together.

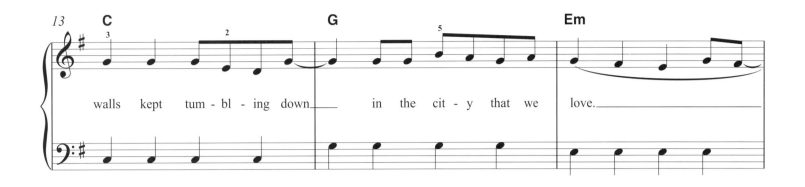

walls kept tum - bl - ing down___ in the cit - y that we love.___

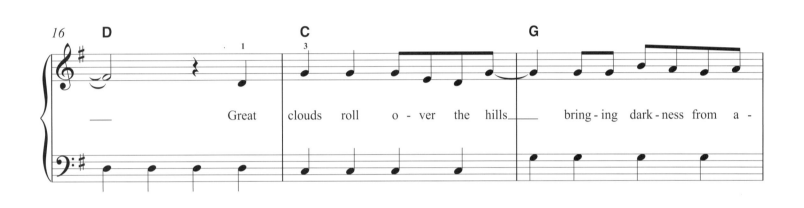

___ Great clouds roll o - ver the hills___ bring - ing dark - ness from a -

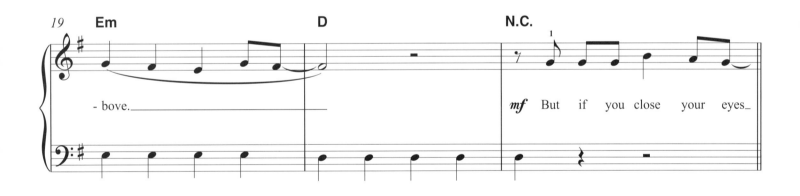

- bove.___ *mf* But if you close your eyes___

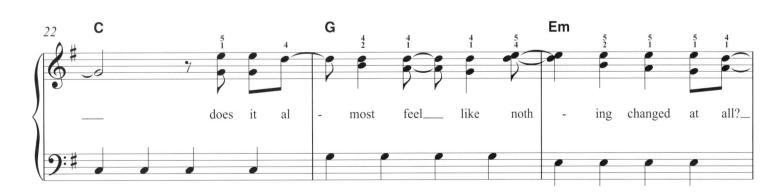

___ does it al - most feel___ like noth - ing changed at all?___

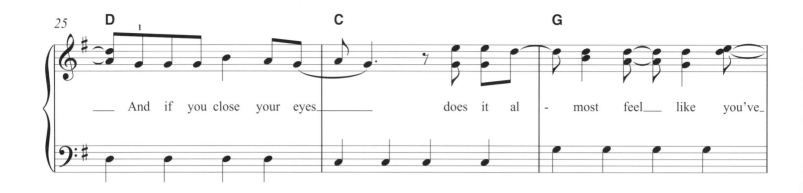

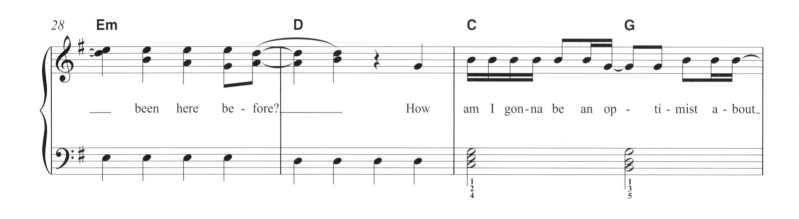

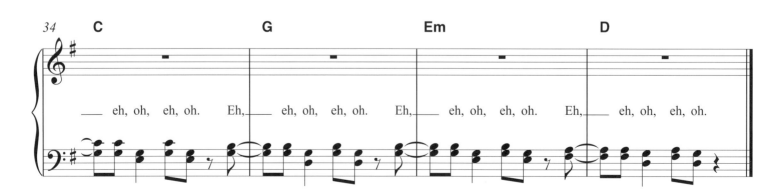

Reach

Words and Music by Cathy Dennis and Andrew Todd

This 2000 track was the fourth single from the squeaky clean pop band, S Club 7. The uplifting track was composed by expert songwriter, Cathy Dennis, who is also responsible for big hits such as Kylie Minogue's 'Can't Get You Out of My Head' and Britney Spears' 'Toxic'. S Club 7 also had their own TV series on CBBC, which ran from 1999 to 2002. The show featured the band trying to get famous, with each series named after the location they would try to find fame in.

Hints & Tips: The melody line is quite low in the verse, in the bass clef. Note the way the right hand moves into the treble clef halfway through the scale at bar 16. Try and maintain the bright, happy nature of this song.

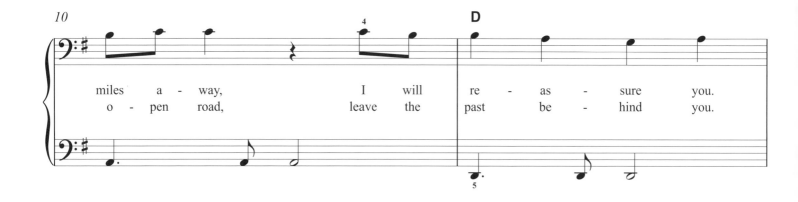

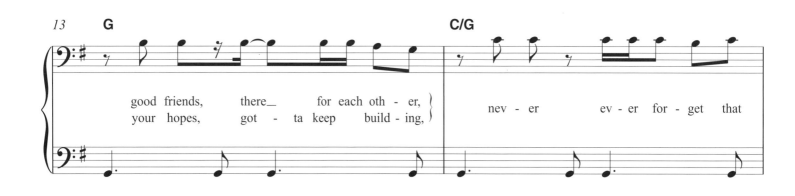

Roar

Words and Music by Katy Perry, Max Martin, Dr. Luke, Bonnie McKee and Henry Walter

As the lead single from Katy Perry's fourth studio album, *Prism*, 'Roar' was a huge international hit for the star, topping the charts in 14 countries including the UK, Australia, Canada, Ireland and New Zealand. Based on the idea of self empowerment and standing up for yourself, the song's video features Perry playing the role of a plane crash survivor in the jungle who learns to conquer her environment by finding her inner tiger.

Hints & Tips: There are lots of instances where both hands have more than one note to play; make sure they all sound together on the correct beat.

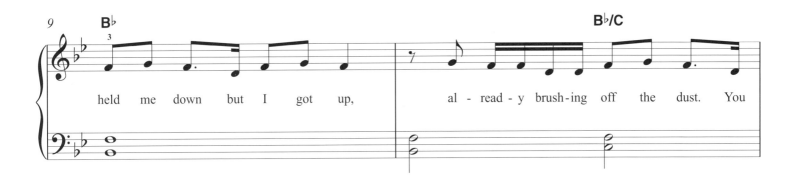

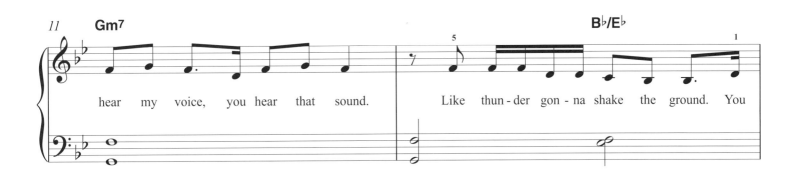

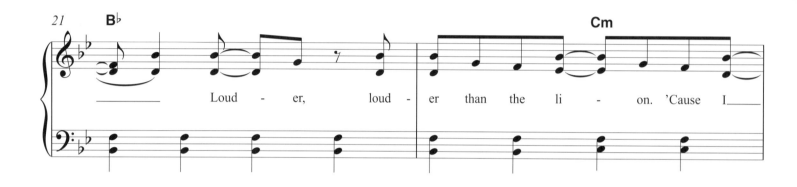

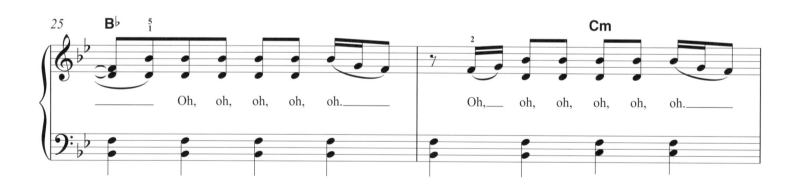

Shake It Off

Words and Music by Taylor Swift, Max Martin and Shellback

The lead single from her fifth studio album, *1989*, went straight to the No. 1 spot on the US Billboard Hot 100.
The lyrics are about Swift learning to not care what the critics or the press say about her, stating
"You can either let it get to you … [or] you just shake it off."

Hints & Tips: During the chorus (from bar 25) the fingering is a little awkward, with the third finger
crossing over the thumb in places. Practise these bits separately until you can play them smoothly.

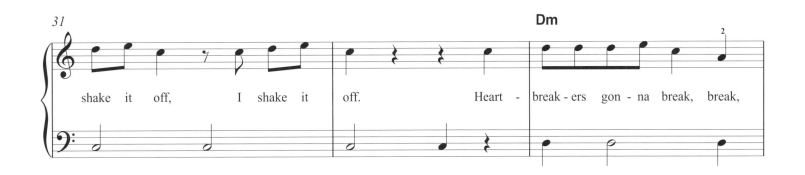

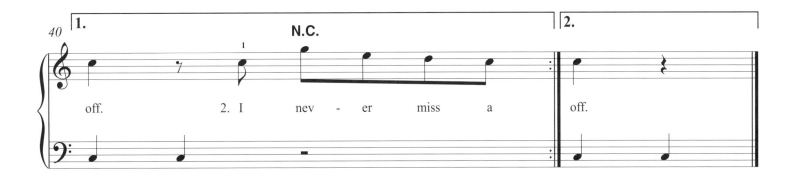

Shotgun

Words and Music by George Barnett, Joel Laslett Pott and Fred Gibson

'Shotgun' is from Ezra's 2018 album, *Staying at Tamara's*, and reached No. 1 in the UK charts. The album is named after the woman whose house Ezra stayed in for a month in Barcelona to wind down from his hectic schedule after the release of his debut album, *Wanted on Voyage*. Released in 2014, *Wanted on Voyage* shot Ezra to fame and was the third highest selling album in the UK that year, following Ed Sheeran and Sam Smith.

Hints & Tips: Both hands share the treble clef at the beginning. In the verse the left hand is very sparse, only playing on beats 2 and 4, but in the chorus it plays on every beat. This produces a 'stomping' effect.

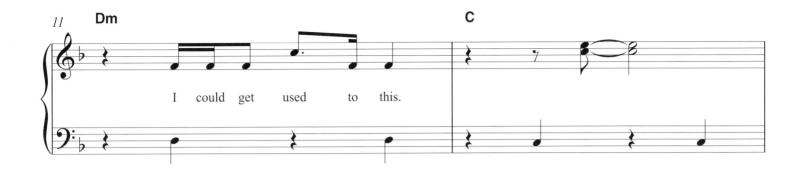

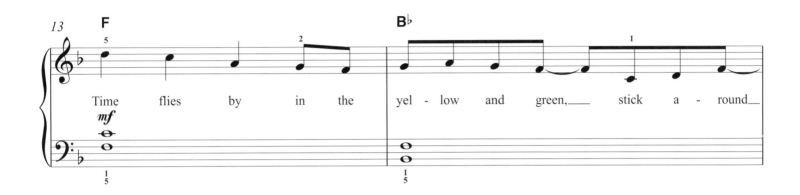

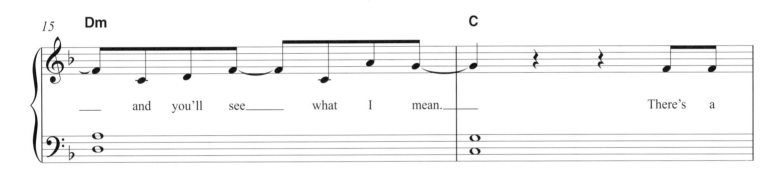

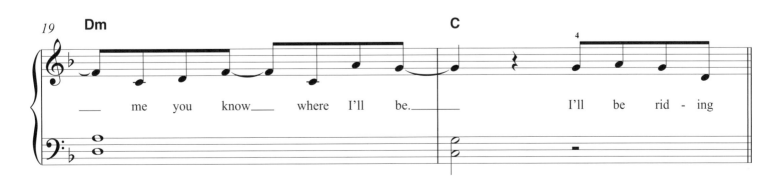

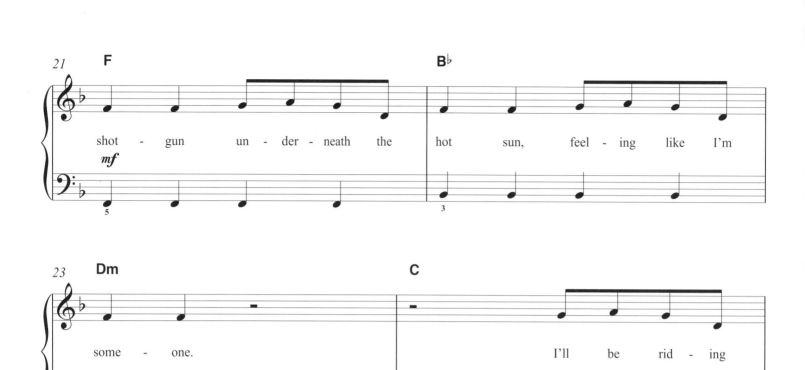

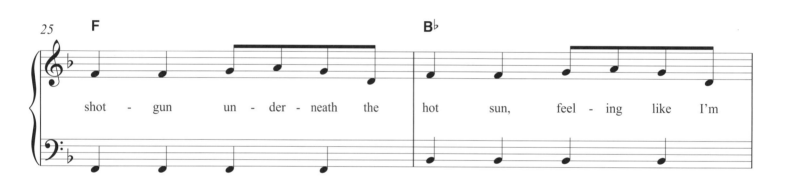

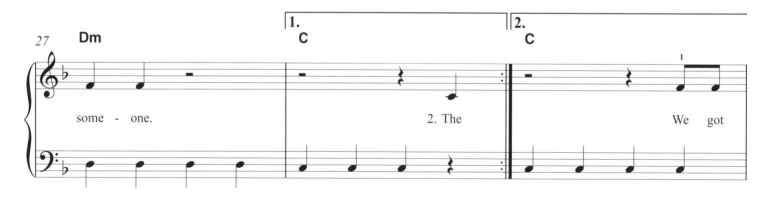

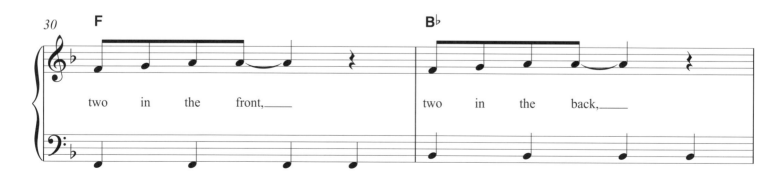

sail - ing a - long_____ and we don't look back._____

Sing

Words and Music by Ed Sheeran and Pharrell Williams

A No. 1 smash hit in the UK, Ireland, Australia, Canada and Israel, 'Sing' was written by Sheeran and Pharrell Williams who also produced the track. As the lead single from *X*, it represented a major departure in the singer-songwriter's sound, moving away from the folk-pop numbers and shifting him more towards R&B. Critics lauded the fresh change in direction, even going as far as to make comparisons between Sheeran and Justin Timberlake.

Hints & Tips: From bar 5 there are different things going on in each hand rhythmically, so practise both thoroughly before putting them together. A metronome will help.

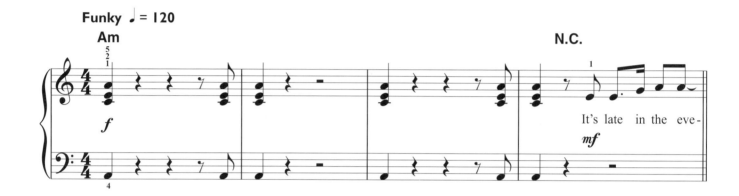

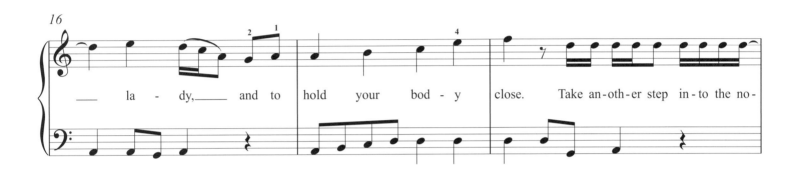

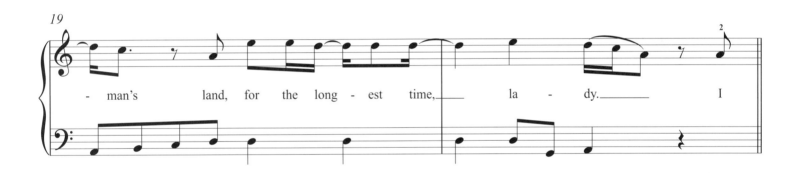

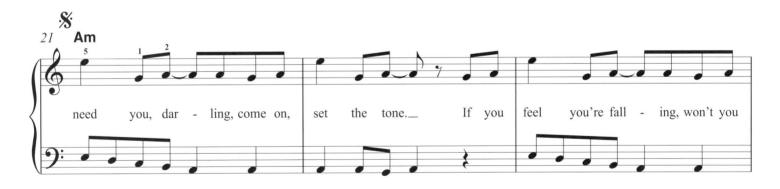

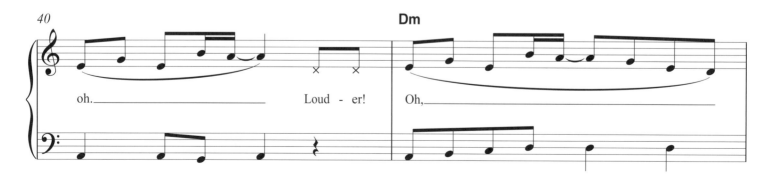

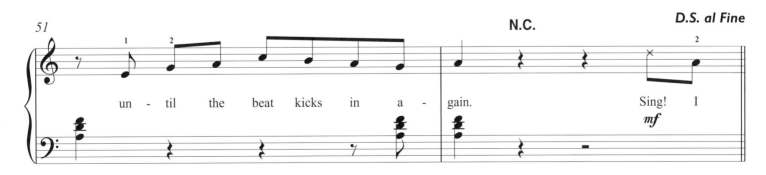

Shut Up and Dance

**Words and Music by Ryan McMahon, Ben Berger,
Sean Waugaman, Eli Maiman, Nicholas Petricca and Kevin Ray**

When frontman Nicholas Petricca was complaining about the drinks line in an LA bar, his friend dragged him away
saying 'shut up and dance with me!'. From this encounter came Walk The Moon's 2014 single, which spent a record 27
weeks at the top of Billboard's Hot Rock Songs. The band wanted to incorporate 80s influences in the track and would take
regular breaks during recording to listen to their favourite 80s hits to keep the sound of the decade fresh in their minds.

Hints & Tips: This is in C major, so you have no sharps or flats to worry about here. However, there are a
lot of repeated Cs in the right hand. Be sure to count carefully and keep a steady pulse. Try it slowly at first.

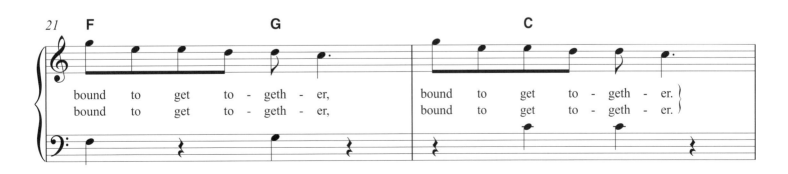

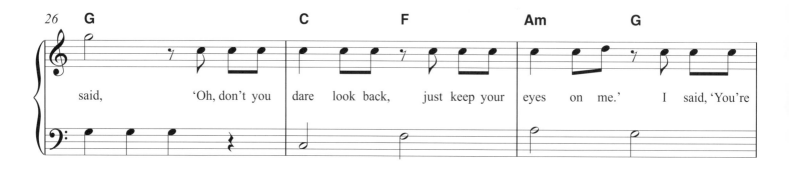

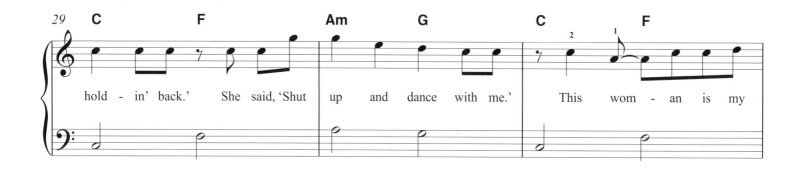

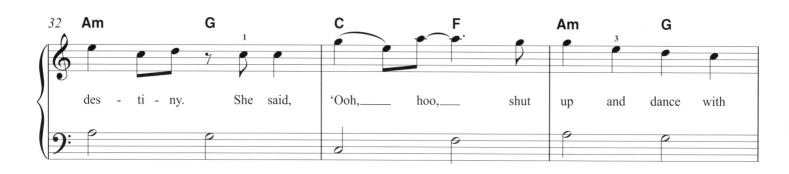

A Sky Full of Stars

Words and Music by Guy Berryman, Jon Buckland, Will Champion, Chris Martin and Tim Bergling

The third single from *Ghost Stories*, co-written and produced by Swedish electronic dance music artist Avicii this is the only dance track on the album and indeed Coldplay's first venture into the genre. On invitation from Chris Martin, Avicii also played piano on the recording.

Hints & Tips: Make sure all the notes that are supposed to be played together sound at exactly the same time, especially in the introduction (bars 1–4).

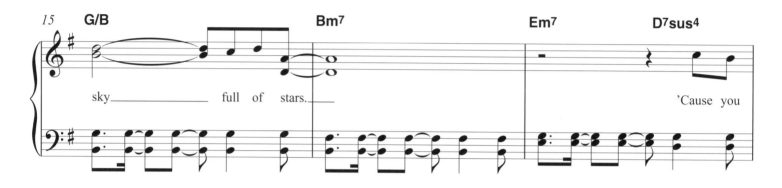

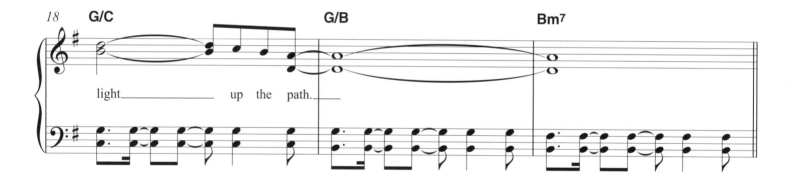

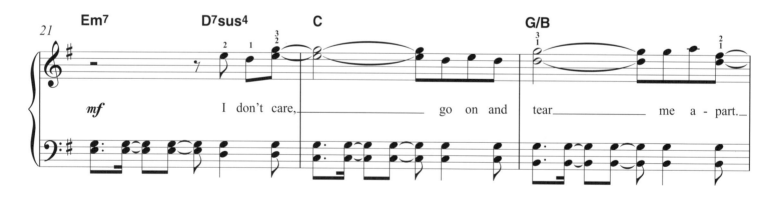

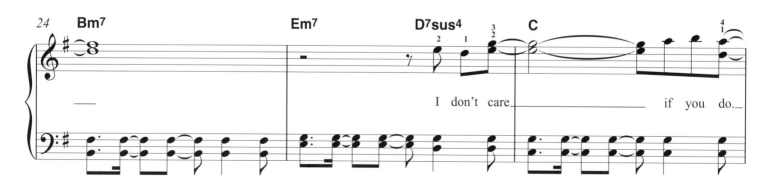

Someone You Loved

Words and Music by Lewis Capaldi, Benjamin Kohn, Peter Kelleher, Thomas Barnes and Samuel Roman

This touching piano ballad about the loss of a loved one is only the second single released by newcomer, Lewis Capaldi, yet it soared to the No. 1 spot! The single was released with a heartwarming music video, starring Capaldi's relative, Peter Capaldi, of *Doctor Who* fame, as a husband who loses his wife and donates her heart to a young mother. The video was made in partnership with the organ donation charity, Live Life Give Life.

Hints & Tips: Practise the left-hand 5ths on their own before adding the right hand.
After that it's much easier. The right hand should be played very *legato*.

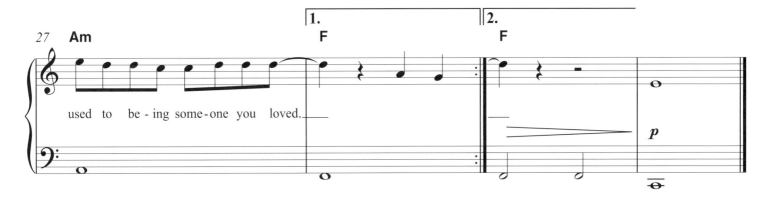

Stitches

Words and Music by Teddy Geiger, Danny Parker and Daniel Kyriakides

This is the third single from Mendes' début album *Handwritten*. It was written by a team before being offered to Mendes, who was reluctant to record a song he didn't write himself, but when he heard it felt a connection to it and knew it was 'the song'. It reached No. 1 in the UK after 17 weeks in the chart, much like Ed Sheeran's 'Thinking Out Loud', which took 19 weeks.

Hints & Tips: There are lots of thirds in the right hand. Be sure to bring your fingers down on the keys at the same time so the notes sound exactly together, and remember the key signature throughout.

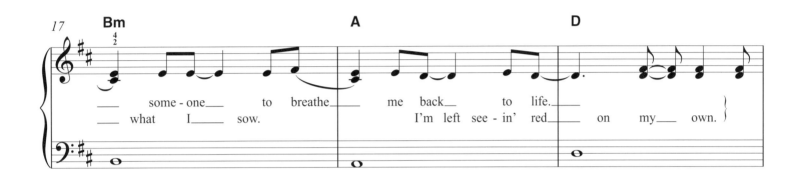

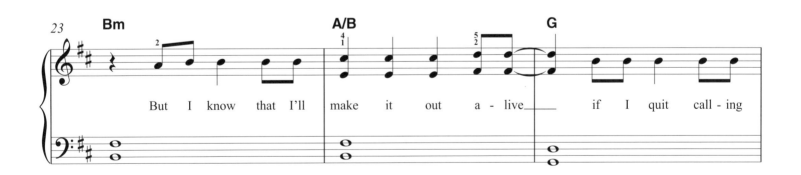

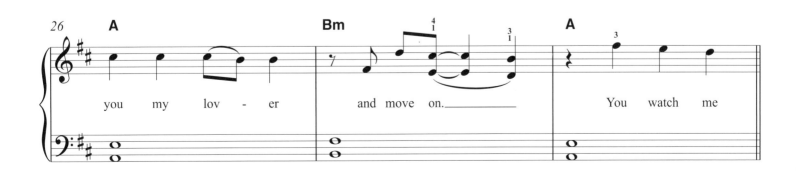

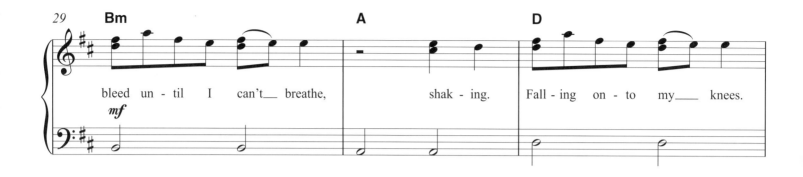

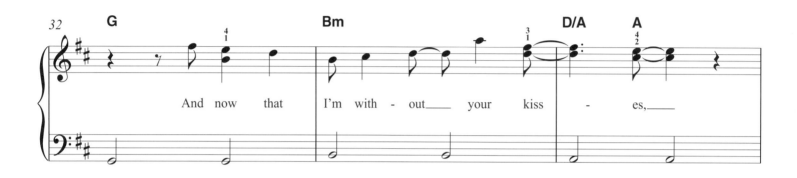

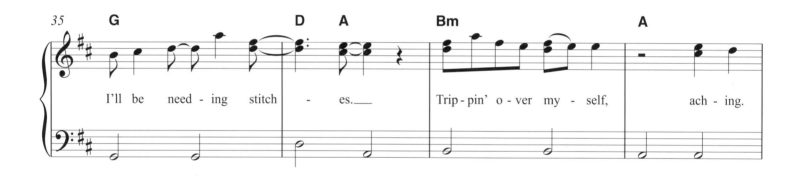

Story of My Life

Words and Music by Jamie Scott, John Henry Ryan, Julian Bunetta, Harry Styles, Liam Payne, Louis Tomlinson, Niall Horan and Zain Malik

This song is seen as a departure from 1D's usual style, being lyrically more intimate and mature. The theme of the song is relationships, past and present, and the more personal nature of the lyrics is owed to the input that Niall, Zayn, Harry, Louis and Liam had on the song. Their own experiences bring this uplifting ballad to life, adding their own ideas to long-time collaborator Jamie Scott's initial song which, when the boys first heard it, caused them to 'freak out' with how great it was.

Hints & Tips: Make sure the octaves (from bar 25) sound exactly together.
If you find it difficult to reach, just play the bottom note each time.

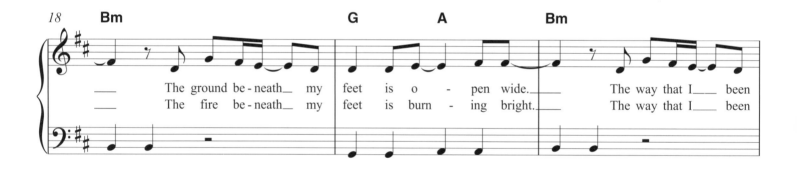

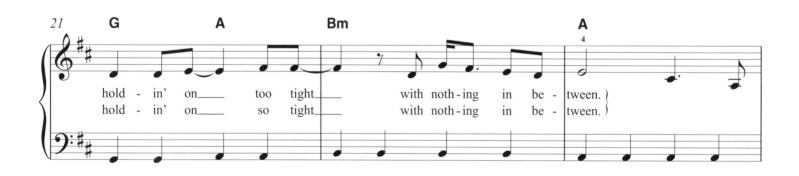

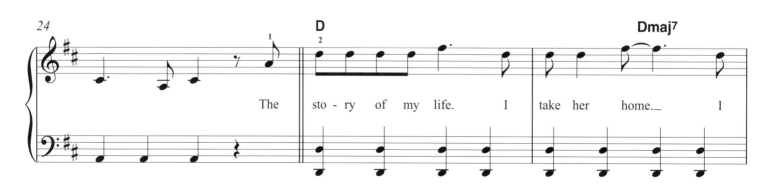

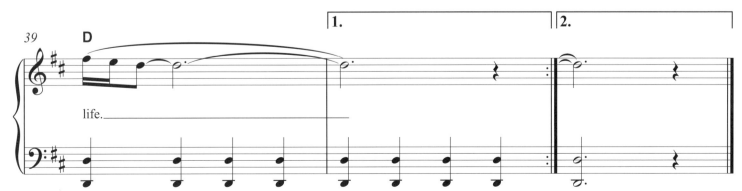

Stronger
(What Doesn't Kill You)

Words and Music by Greg Kurstin, Alexandra Tamposi, David Gamson and Jorgen Elofsson

The winner of the first *American Idol* in 2002, Kelly Clarkson has had a long and successful career as a powerhouse singer. With previous singles including her 2003 hit 'Miss Independent' and pop-rock anthem 'Since U Been Gone' in 2004, this track falls in line with Clarkson's signature empowering singalong-style tunes. It is included in her fifth album, *Stronger* which was released in 2011 and was inspired by Nietzsche's quote, 'That which does not kill us makes us stronger'.

Hints & Tips: Keep it soft at the beginning, only building up to forte at the start of the chorus. Here the left hand plays on every beat, driving the music forward.

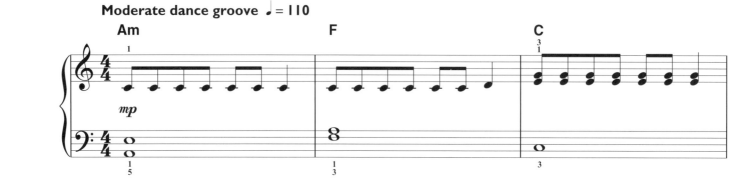

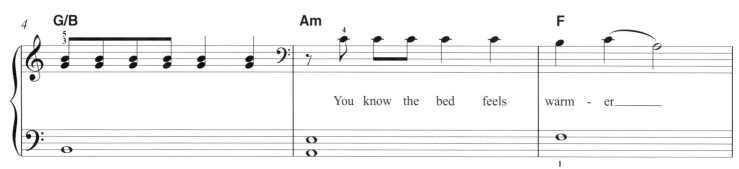

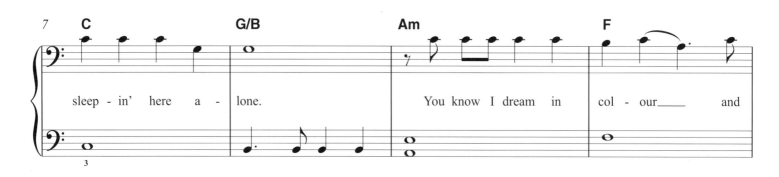

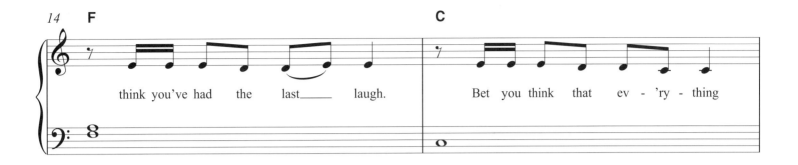

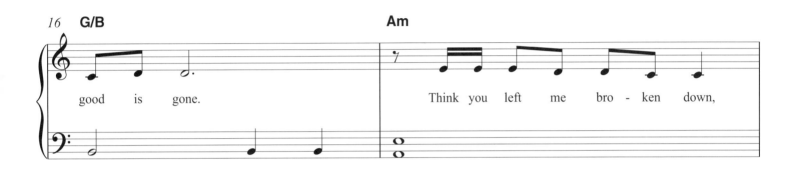

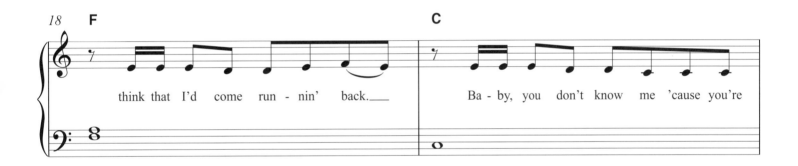

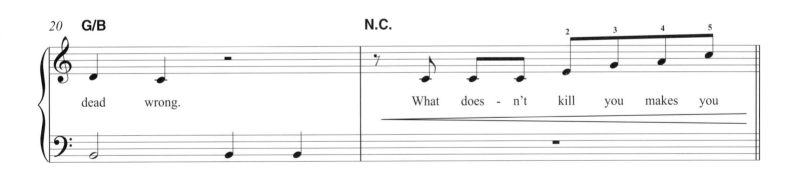

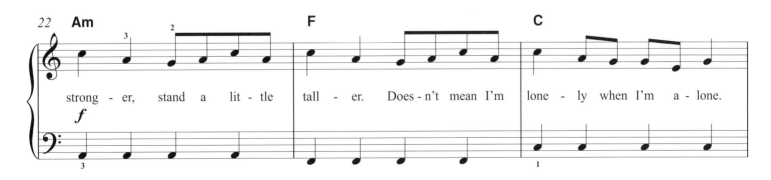

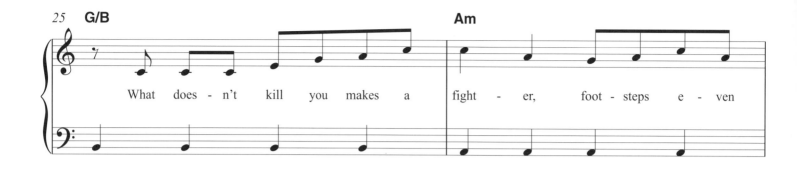

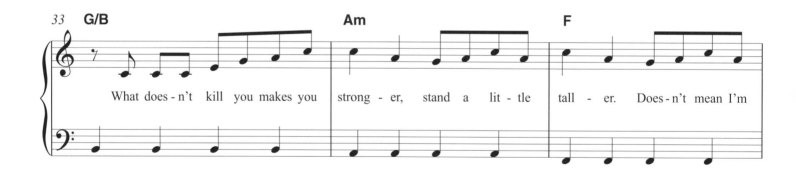

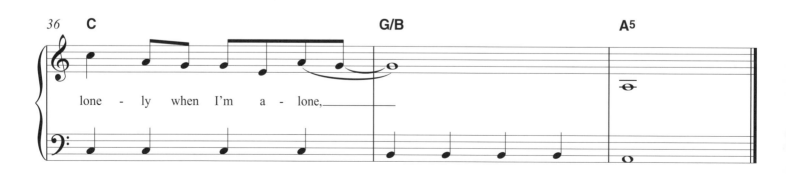

Uptown Funk

Words and Music by Mark Ronson, Bruno Mars, Philip Lawrence, Jeff Bhasker, Devon Gallaspy, Nicholaus Williams, Lonnie Simmons, Ronnie Wilson, Charles Wilson, Rudolph Taylor and Robert Wilson

'Uptown Funk!' was in the charts at the same time as Vance Joy's 'Riptide'. Both songs mention actress Michelle Pfeiffer, though for different reasons: 'Uptown Funk!' makes reference to her role in the movie *Scarface*, while Vance Joy was simply a fan of hers when he was younger.

Hints & Tips: The melody of this song is quite repetitive. Make it more interesting by trying to play it percussively, for example, experimenting with articulation, adding *staccato* etc.

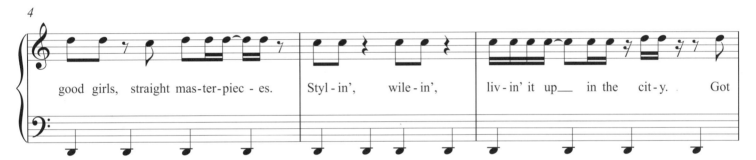

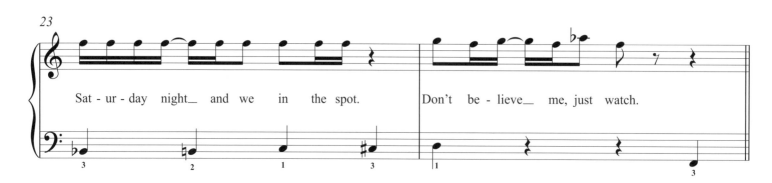

We Are Young

Words and Music by Jeff Bhasker, Andrew Dost, Jack Antonoff and Nate Ruess

When the talented musicians that make up the band Fun formed in 2008, it was only a year later that their first album, *Aim and Ignite*, was released. 'We Are Young' appears on the band's second album *Some Nights*, released a few years later in 2012. The song is about the joy of being young and having a night out to remember and features vocalist Janelle Monae. It became the most listened to song on Facebook in the year of its release!

Hints & Tips: The right-hand melody line should sound conversational in the verse — don't worry too much about the exact rhythms here. At the start of the chorus your hands are quite far apart: If you struggle with this you could try playing the left hand an octave higher.

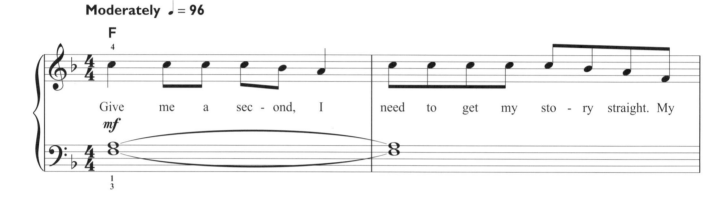

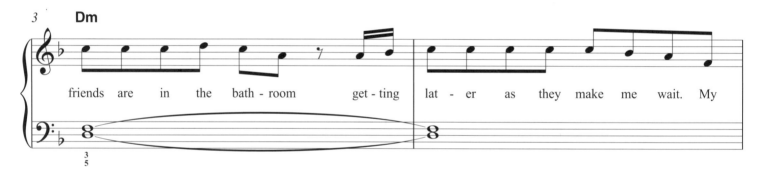

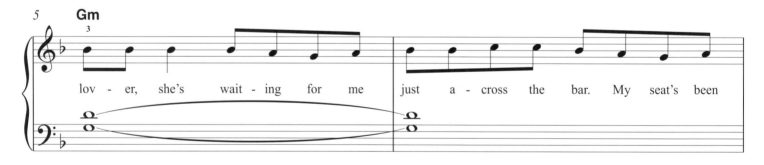

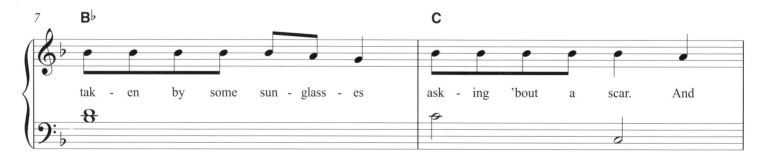

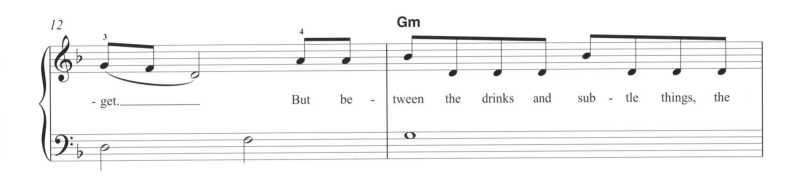

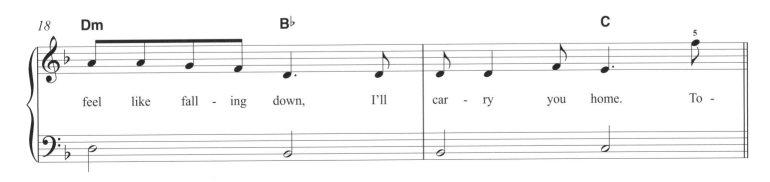

What Makes You Beautiful

Words and Music by Savan Kotecha, Rami Yacoub and Carl Falk

The success of this song helped to propel One Direction into becoming one of the biggest pop acts around, conquering the USA and the head of a new British Invasion. At the 2012 BRIT Awards, the band's success was recognised with the trophy for Best British Single, an award that was soon joined by gongs from the MTV Video Music Awards and Teen Choice Awards.

Hints & Tips: Don't be tempted to hold down the left-hand notes too long; the rests should be given the full count.

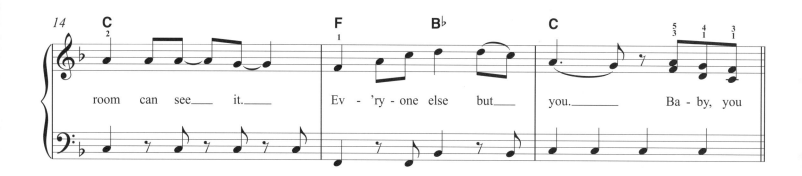

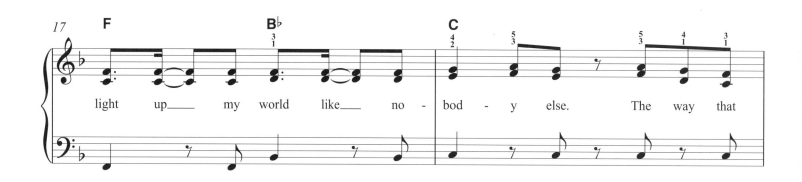

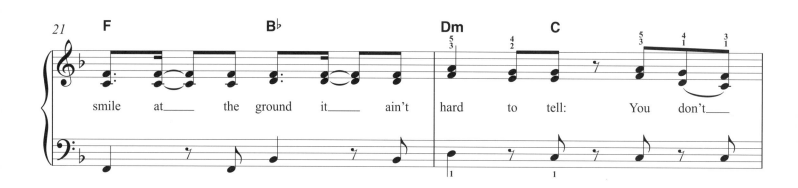

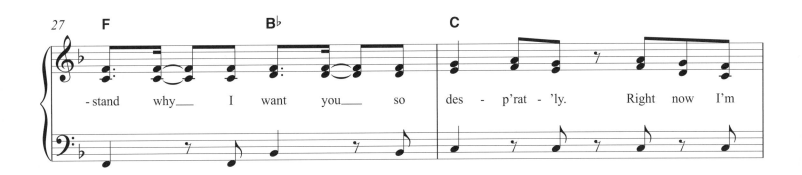

This Is Me
from THE GREATEST SHOWMAN

Words and Music by Benj Pasek and Justin Paul

This smash hit from the 2017 film, *The Greatest Showman*, is sung by Keala Settle, who plays bearded woman, Lettie Lutz, in the movie. 'This Is Me' was written by Benj Pasek and Justin Paul and speaks about self-acceptance in the face of oppression, becoming the anthem of a film that celebrates the diversity of people. The powerful song won the Golden Globe for Best Original Song in 2018.

Hints & Tips: Make sure you are familiar with the key signature; there are a few places in the right hand where the C♯s could catch you out.

they say, no one -'ll love_ you as_ you_ are._ But

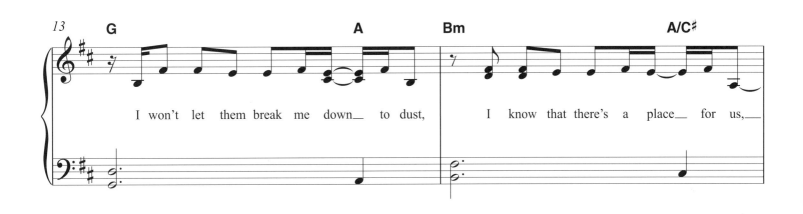

I won't let them break me down_ to dust, I know that there's a place_ for us,_

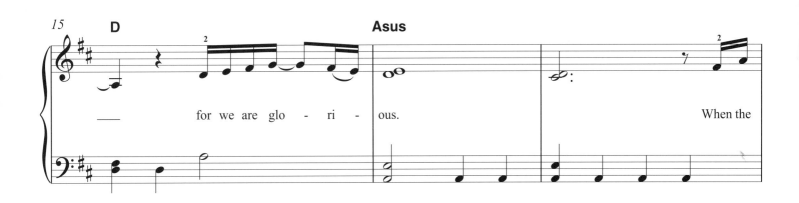

for we are glo - ri - ous. When the

sharp - est words_ wan - na cut me down,_ I'm gon - na

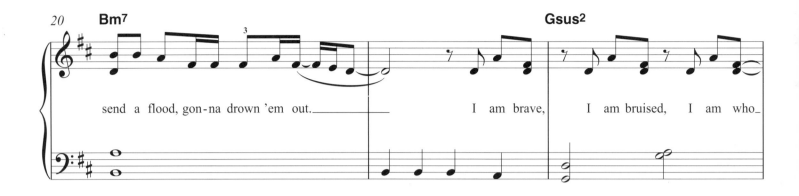

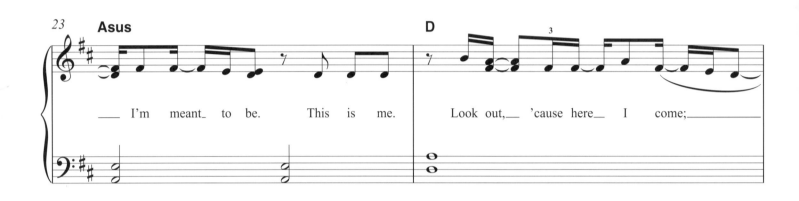

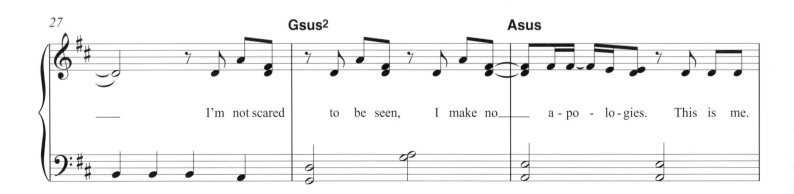

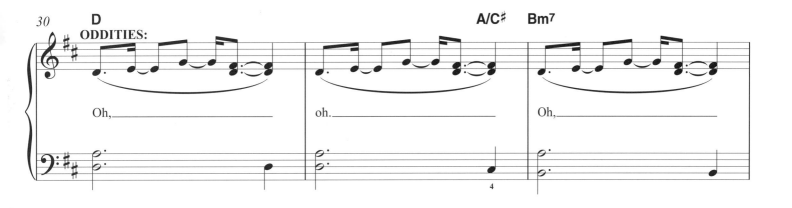

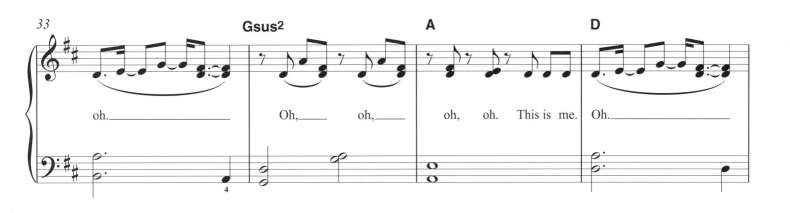

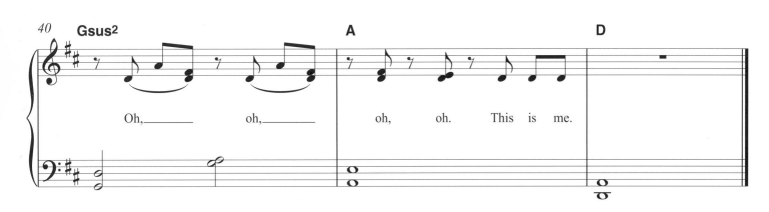

Discover our range of really easy piano bumper books...

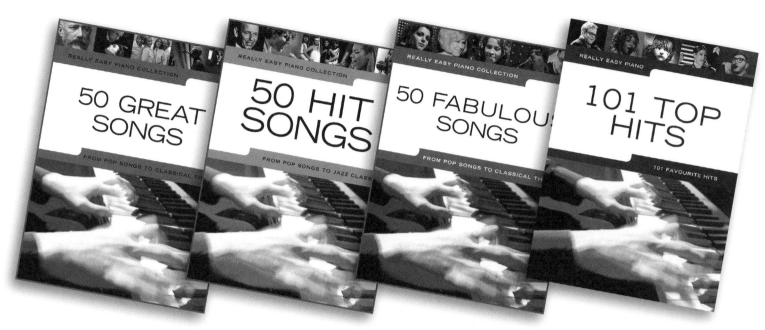

ORDER NO. AM995643   ORDER NO. AM1000615   ORDER NO. AM999449   ORDER NO. AM1008975

ORDER NO. HLE90004915   ORDER NO. AM1011032   ORDER NO. HL00295382   ORDER NO. HL00287156

Just visit your local music shop and ask
to see our huge range of music in print.